Whole Brain
Learning and Teaching

A practical introduction
for learners of all ages,
parents and teachers.

Dr. John Kelly

Printed by CreateSpace

Published by Fingerprint Learning Limited

Copyright © 2016 by John Kelly

LEGAL NOTICE: All rights reserved. No part of this publication may be reproduced, stored in a retrieval system, or transmitted in any form or by any means, electronic, mechanical, photocopying, scanning, recording or otherwise, without the prior written permission of the copyright owner of this book.

The author has asserted his rights under Section 77 of the Copyright, Designs and Patents Act, 1988 UK, to be identified as the author of this book.

First edition 2016.
Available on Kindle and other online stores.
Available from Amazon.com, Amazon.uk, Amazon's other European websites and other retail outlets.
Available from Fingerprint Learning Limited.

Information about Fingerprint Learning can be found at www.fingerprintlearning.com
Inquiries about Fingerprint Learning Programmes can be made to info@fingerprintlearning.com
or
Fingerprint Learning Ltd,
15 Grays Hill , Bangor,
N. Ireland, United Kingdom
BT20 3BB

ISBN-13: 978-1522824749
ISBN-10: 152282474X

ACKNOWLEDGMENTS

I owe so much to parents, teachers, friends and colleagues who have read sections of the manuscript for this book and made helpful suggestions and corrections. I also owe an enormous debt to those who have pioneered in the area of learning styles and whole brain approaches to learning and teaching. I have learnt so much from their work, some of which is represented in the Reading List at the end of this book. I hope that I have attributed all relevant quotations and references to them correctly.

I am particularly indebted to Stephanie Conn and Dr. Brian Cummins for extensively reviewing and improving the text and its layout. Although the final responsibility for the content is mine alone, their suggested improvements have been invaluable. My thanks are also due to Dr. Ian Taylor for assisting me with the process of self-publishing and who, with Ross McConaghy, helped with the design and layout of the cover.

"...the individuality inherent in our brain networks makes that of fingerprints or facial features gross and simple by comparison."
Roger W. Sperry.
Nobel Prize Winner for Physiology and Medicine, 1981.

This book is dedicated to my children,
Wendy-Ann, Sarah, Patrick and Ruth,
who have taught me that, in education,
one size does not fit all.

CONTENTS

Fore-words

Introduction   1

1 Is the Revolution Passing You By?   8

2 Learning in Infancy and at Primary Level   22

3 Discovering the 'Grain of your Brain'   27

4 *Smarter* Learning for *better* Learning   41

5 21st Century Education for 21st Century Learners   46

6 Fear, Failure—and Fun!   49

7 The Adolescent Brain   56

8 Sensory Learning Preferences or VA(T)K   63

9 Two Brains in One   73

10 Cooperation or Conflict?   85

11 Learning and Memory   91

12 Conclusion: Let's *Do* Something Now!   99

Reading List   103

The Fingerprint Learning for Life Programme   104

Progressive Whole Brain Plans for Schools   105

About the Author   111

FORE-WORDS
Responses to the Fingerprint Learning Workshops

Individuals
"They helped me to understand how my brain works and how to get the most out of it."

"I have learned techniques that show me the best way to record and learn my work"

"The programme made me realise that as a young mother I have a range of skills and knowledge that can aid me in future employment."

"Knowing my learning style has helped me notice that I work better at a desk with music and I have a strong memory for pictures and images. I like to know the reason why I am learning a certain subject. Now that I understand these things about myself, I can learn more effectively."

Teachers
"The education system is not addressing the multiple learning abilities of our children."

"All pupils are different, learn differently and should be treated as individuals."

"Poor behaviour may be as a result of learning techniques going against the 'grain' of brain."

A School Principal
"Fingerprint Learning's approach to Smartnesses has been the single most significant initiative in the life of the school for building self-awareness and self-esteem within our pupils and community."

Parents
"It made me know that I can be a better dad."

"It helped me realise I can help my child learn."

INTRODUCTION

Learning is for life!
The *Transforming Futures Series* of books is about Learning for Life. This phrase has a double meaning that indicates that learning can enhance and enrich your quality of life—and that it should also be a lifelong experience. The value and benefits of learning are enduring and apply to every person at every stage of life. I hope that the series will inform, enthuse and motivate you about the wonderful capacity we all have to learn throughout our lives and how understanding the process can help us to become more effective learners.

Learning is something that our brains do naturally. From the first moments after birth a baby's brain is learning as it processes the massive amount of stimulation coming through its senses. Learning will be a daily experience and eventually more formal education in Nursery and in School will begin to influence the learning process. Of course, learning involves more than education, but in our society formal education plays a major role in learning. While this can be a positive influence that enhances the learning experience, for some it can be a negative experience, in which difficulties in formal education discourage learning—or at least undermine confidence that one can learn successfully.

Every career involves further learning experiences and this is more evident today than ever because people are unlikely to remain in one career throughout their life. Most people will change their jobs many times throughout their working life and in each case there will be more learning to do. Even those who remain in the same career will experience changes in their work demands and this means learning to adapt to change. Work and lifelong learning will travel hand in hand for most people.

Ideally, learning should continue well beyond retirement and into the final phase of our lives. That phase can now last for thirty or more years and the quality of those years can be significantly enhanced by further learning. However, there is more to learning in later life than improving the quality of life. It may be a matter of *survival* as well. From a medical perspective, lifelong learning is becoming a necessity if the increasing incidence of dementia and depression in retirement is to be reversed. The changes in the brain associated Alzheimer's disease begin twenty years before the onset of symptoms. Lifelong learning builds what is known as *cognitive reserve* in your brain and is the most effective way to delay or prevent dementia. Mental decline is not inevitable if we continue to keep our brains stimulated with appropriate learning. With your brain, if you *use it* you are much less likely to *lose it*.

For this reason alone whole communities need to place a higher premium on the importance of learning at every stage of life. A revolution in how we view learning and engage with it is required if this is to happen. This book is therefore about a *learning revolution*—and the benefits that can accompany it.

The idea for this series was conceived in three articles I wrote for the Belfast Telegraph on the Brain and Learning in 2014. The material in each of the chapters has been presented to hundreds of adults and young people through Fingerprint Learning Workshops since 2007—with universally encouraging responses. The Workshops have been delivered to children as young as 11 years old to adults in their 90s. They have involved business people and students, teachers and trainers, unemployed adults and 'residents' in Her Majesty's Prisons. I hope that making the material more widely available will contribute to strategies and techniques for learning that already exist. In particular, it will introduce you to the organ of learning in the body—your brain—and how you can use it to learn more effectively yourself, as well understand how others learn and how to help them learn too.

Over the last twenty five years amazing discoveries have been made about how the brain learns. This has transformed our understanding of *how* we learn and what is happening *when* we learn as well as when we don't learn sometimes. These insights should be making a revolutionary impact on all teaching, training and mentoring—but have they? As you read on you will find out how much you know about these developments and how much you have missed out on until now.

This book is 'what it says on the tin'—*a practical introduction to whole brain learning and teaching for learners of all ages, parents and teachers.* I want to stress its relevance to *all learners*, even though I have specifically provided practical applications for teachers and parents in the education of children and young people. Whoever you are and whatever your age there will be something for you in these chapters.

It is about *whole brain learning and teaching.* The brain has been created as the *organ of learning* in the body. Therefore

- *learning* will be more successful when the learner knows how to use this organ of learning efficiently.
- *teaching and training* is more likely to be effective when it is delivered with an understanding how the brain learns.

Understanding the ways in which the brain learns can overcome barriers to learning due to negative experiences in education. It can convince us that *everyone can learn and learn successfully.*

It is a *practical introduction for learners of all ages, parents and teachers.* In the category of *teachers* I include school teachers, university and college lecturers, trainers, mentors and coaches, youth workers and anyone engaged in teaching other people.

- It is *practical*—inasmuch as it is intended for day to day use rather than as a theoretical treatise on education.
- It is *an introduction* to aspects of teaching and learning which many people, including teachers, may not be familiar with. Although much has already been written about some of the themes in this book, such as learning styles, most people have not yet been introduced to *the role of the brain* in learning and to what I call *whole brain* learning and teaching.

- It is about *learning and teaching* because these should be two sides of one coin. We all know from our own school experience that teaching does not always lead to learning. Most of us could agree that the emphasis on *what* we were expected to learn in formal education vastly outweighed any instruction we received on *how* to learn it.

- It is relevant for *learners of all ages* in a wide variety of contexts because effective learning and teaching affects us all and, in one sense, we will all have some role to play as teachers and learners throughout our lives. I have written for **teachers** in the light of what I have learnt from training hundreds of teachers in Fingerprint Workshops. Since *parents* have a vital role in teaching their children as well as in cooperating with school teachers, I have also written with them in mind.

Whole Brain Learning and Teaching is intended for use more as a *manual or handbook than a textbook*. In order to obtain my medical degree I had to remember a vast amount of information for the Finals examination. I studied numerous volumes on each branch of Medicine and had six years' worth of knowledge to assimilate and recall.

On my first day in the wards as a practising doctor, all my study was reduced to a small medical book in the pocket of my white coat. This was a brief handbook on Medicine which I consulted frequently in caring for patients on the wards on a day to day basis. I was struck by the contrast between the tomes I had to master for an exam and what I needed for day to day medical practice as a junior houseman on the wards.

Teaching and learning is a vast theme which involves psychology, specific subject information, curriculum development and planning, pedagogy and assessment. However, there are simple principles and practices that can be used by us all, including parents and young people. The aim of this manual is to make some of these readily accessible for everyday use, so I hope you will treat this book like my medical pocketbook—as a practical handbook to dip into and, above all, to use in practice. In other words, I hope you will find yourself returning to it frequently once you have read it through.

The aim of this book is to
- *inform and enthuse you* about the exciting discoveries concerning the brain and learning.
- *apply* them in interesting and practical ways to teaching and learning in your own environment, whether in work, home, school, college or in business.
- *motivate* you to get involved in lifelong learning and engage with the *learning revolution* that has emerged in the last twenty five years due to understanding how our brains learn.

The second and third books in the series will apply whole brain learning to **Mental Wellbeing in Retirement** and to **Business Management,** respectively. The series title **Transforming Futures** expresses the conviction that *effective learning* can be transforming for everyone in every sphere of life and at every stage of life.

Learning is easier when you know your learning 'fingerprint'
Formal education in most schools has been described as a 'one size fits all' approach. Apart from some exceptional cases, pupils and students are taught the *same* curriculum in the *same* way and their learning is assessed in the *same* way. However, as this book clearly illustrates, we are not all the same and we do not learn in identical ways. The exciting discoveries about how the brain is 'wired to learn' has revealed that, in the words of Roger Sperry, winner of the Nobel Prize for Physiology and Medicine (1981),

'The more we learn, the more we recognise the unique complexity of any one human intellect, the stronger the conclusion becomes that the individuality inherent in our brain networks makes that of fingerprints or facial features gross and simple by comparison.'

We have described this as your *learning fingerprint*. Every brain is wired to learn, but not every brain is wired in the same way.

In other words, we learn in different ways. So why are we still teaching and assessing people in the same ways? My experience suggests that when learners and teachers understand how learning takes place in the brain, the experience of teaching and learning can be made less difficult and much more enjoyable.

When I was in an airport recently I was struck by how few people carry a suitcase any more. Almost everyone uses suitcases that are like trolleys – with handles and wheels. Anyone carrying a suitcase stands out today. The 20th century was the century for carrying suitcases. The 21st century is for mobile suitcases. So much educational practice and assessment is still in 20th century mode, like carrying suitcases. It gets a job done, but it is out of date. The new discoveries about how the brain learns are truly revolutionary and should be fundamental to 21st century teaching – but are not.

Let me give another example to show I am not exaggerating. If you visited a physiotherapist and asked her how long she had trained, she would probably say that it had taken about four years. Suppose you asked how many lectures she had received on bones, joints, muscles and nerves during the four years. If she replied that she had not had any, would you be surprised?

Which organ of the body do teachers work with every day in teaching and learning? The brain, of course. How many lectures do teachers on Initial Teacher Education receive? When I put this question to teachers in Fingerprint Learning Workshops the answer is usually, "None". The only exception has been in early years' education. Yet the discoveries that have been made into the brain as the organ of learning should have led to entire modules, not just lectures, on the how the brain learns. What you read in this book should be part of the abc's of teacher education and I hope, when you have finished it, you will agree.

I was once a General Practitioner, or GP. I did not specialize in any branch of Medicine, but I knew a lot about the body in general and how it worked. I kept up to date with new developments and discoveries that would help me be a more effective practitioner of Medicine. I believe that all teachers are *Learning Practitioners*—LPs, if you like. They are the practitioners of learning in our communities. They deserve to know all that is available about the organ of learning they are seeking to influence. It is to them that parents should be able to turn for advice and expertise about how to help their children learn successfully. This should involve being kept up to date on how the brain learns and the best ways to enable it to do so. It should be central to teacher training and professional development—but it isn't. So, if you are a parent or teacher, this book will challenge you to do something about this.

When our education system engages with this revolution,
- our schools will be very different from what they are at present.
- Governments will be setting different educational priorities.
- teacher training will be revolutionised.
- more young people will emerge from formal education as experienced and accomplished learners.

As you will discover in the final chapter, I have written this book as a challenge to the status quo in Education today. It is a challenge to all of us, including parents and teachers, to bring Education from the 20th century into the 21st century.

How to read this book
Having introduced you to the underlying motivation for this book on teaching and learning, I will offer some suggestions on *how to read it*.
- Please don't assume you should read from front to back. Look at the chapter headings, or even skip through the book, and start with what catches your eye. You might be more interested in the section on adolescence, or your attention might be drawn to the chapter on the 'grain of the brain', or to the chapter about practical tips on Smarter Learning.

- Many of the chapters end with *Top Tips* for effective teaching and learning. This section includes a *Checklist* for you to review your own experience, especially as a parent or teacher. The Checklist is followed by some Tips on how to apply the information in the preceding chapter.

- Enjoy it! If a chapter you are reading seems like heavy going, turn to another part of the book and return to the more challenging sections later. We all learn more when we enjoy the experience of learning, and this book is intended to be an enjoyable learning experience for you.

You will not encounter anything that has not been written about in more detail by others. I have benefited from the work of many others who have written on specific themes covered in **Whole Brain Learning and Teaching**. I have tried to bring together many of these approaches to create a 'One Stop Shop' where you can sample various aspects of brain-based learning. You may be encouraged to explore some of the subjects I have covered in more depth for yourself, and the Reading List will guide you in doing so. If you are a teacher, it may prompt you to recall useful information or practices you learnt in College and had forgotten about, or never got around to using.

Writing **Whole Brain Learning and Teaching** will have been worthwhile if I am able to introduce you to the revolution in learning that has been taking place in the last twenty five years! I will be even more satisfied if I can persuade you that this has the potential to transform your future and the future of those around you.

CHAPTER 1

Is the Revolution Passing You By?

We are living in a Revolution that is changing the way we live, communicate, think and prosper.
Dryden and Vos, The Learning Revolution, 2001

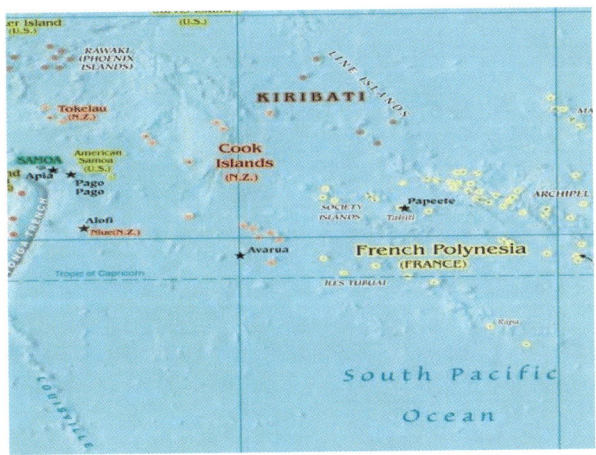

This chapter focuses on the 'big picture' in which education takes place. If you look at this map to find the names of *specific* islands in the Pacific Ocean you may fail to notice the words 'South Pacific Ocean' on the page. You might see the details but miss the wider context. When we survey the realm of education there can be a similar focus on specific aspects of education while we miss the big picture. For instance, it is possible to focus on literacy and numeracy, Key Stage Assessment and SATS, on Transfer testing, Special Educational Needs and so on, but broader aspects of what education and learning is really about may be missed altogether. The brain is the *organ* in the body where all learning takes place. To consider education and by-pass the role of the brain will be like missing the 'Pacific Ocean', in which *specific aspects* of education are located.

This book locates different aspects of successful learning in the broader context of how the brain learns, or, in a term I will explain later, 'the grain of the brain'. In other words, I hope to present the 'Pacific Ocean' of what learning is, as well as identify some of the more important 'islands' located in it. I hope you will find this perspective on education as interesting as I have and that it will prompt you to think about it in new and exciting ways as a learner, parent or teacher.

In the Introduction I mentioned that as a General Practitioner I did not specialise in a single branch of Medicine but I knew a lot about the human body for the purposes of General Medicine. I was a *practitioner* of Medicine, seeking to improve the physical and mental wellbeing of my patients. This is why I like to describe teachers as *learning practitioners* and not just practitioners of *teaching*. Although I believe that everyone who is engaged in teaching and learning is a learning practitioner, those who are teaching *professionals* have a unique role in our community. They are people who have been trained to teach and so can be expected to understand what effective learning involves. Schools should therefore be central 'hubs' of *learning* as well as places of *teaching*, where other people who are engaged in teaching in the home and in the community can be equipped by professionals to become better learning practitioners. These statements imply a number of personal convictions.

- Firstly, teaching and learning are not the same thing. This is a crucially important distinction. All of us have only *learnt* a small fraction of the vast amount of *teaching* we have been exposed to throughout our lives.

- Secondly, professional teachers are not the only practitioners of learning in our communities. Anyone who helps others to learn what they have already learnt themselves—through teaching, training or mentoring—is a practitioner of learning. Parents, grandparents, non-paid instructors, religious instructors and youth workers are included in this description.
- Thirdly, we should expect teachers, as professional learning practitioners, to be the people who *not only understand how learning takes place but can impart* this understanding to others in the non-professional categories I have just mentioned.
- Fourthly, there could be no higher vocation in our society than to be a professional learning practitioner. Seriously! How can we place a value on the skill of helping others to learn and to understand what effective learning is for themselves. To be able to teach is valuable, but to have *the skill to enable others to learn* is even more valuable. Learning practitioners should be valued for their ability to this—and all the more so when they are given the opportunity to share this skill with others.
- Fifthly, it should be taken for granted that, just as General Practitioners have a working knowledge of the human body, professional learning practitioners would have a working knowledge of the organ of learning in the body—the brain.

There have been times in our society when the teaching profession was held in similar esteem to medical practitioners. Teachers were accorded much higher honour as practitioners of learning than they are today.

Today the role of the teacher as a learning practitioner needs to be restored to this position of honour and respect in our society because *they are the people who help us understand what learning is about*. In the 21st century this implies that they are the people in our community who can explain how the brain learns—and share this understanding with others.

The books in the **Transforming Futures** series are about how a *vision* for education, teaching and learning can transform the future of
- every learner
- teaching as a profession
- our community

Never before has a *vision for learning* been more important. In a world of such rapid change the ability to keep on learning throughout our lives has become a necessity rather than a luxury.

Consider two examples:

Firstly, remaining in one occupation for a lifetime has become exceptional. Most people will have a number of jobs and careers throughout their working life or will be expected to deal with considerable change within their job. As a result of this they will have to learn new skills and information more frequently and continuously than in the past. This places a premium on *knowing how to learn* to adapt to new work opportunities and be equipped to take them. Teaching someone how to learn is equipping him or her for the rapidly changing world of work and not just the initial step of getting a job for life. Schools need to become places where young people are learning to learn and not just learning to pass examinations and gain qualifications to get access to jobs.

Secondly, the rising incidence of dementia and mental decline is related to the degree to which people have built up the 'cognitive reserve' in their brains through continued learning throughout life. This cognitive reserve is like building up a retirement fund in your brain which can be drawn upon as you age. While some dementias are genetic and unavoidable, mental decline is not inevitable and the incidence of dementia can be dramatically reduced when people keep learning for life and build up this reserve. There is increasing evidence of people with Alzheimer's changes in their brains who did not develop the symptoms of dementia during their lives. Lifelong learning is the healthiest activity for the brain. If you *use it* you are less likely to *lose it*!

These are only two of the reasons why a vision for learning is so important today. We will come to a third reason shortly. It involves the revolution in our understanding of learning that has taken place in the last twenty five years due to amazing discoveries about how the brain learns. Nothing could be more *envisioning* than to have a role in applying these discoveries to advance a revolution in teaching and learning in the 21st century.

I hope that reading this book will introduce you to this revolution and inspire you to get involved in promoting it wherever you have influence—among your friends, in your family, in schools and colleges and other spheres of life such as business and sport. There is no part of life which cannot be influenced by this vision for 21st century learning. Let's look at why this is so.

It is unlikely that anybody in our society today has been able to avoid the impact of the Digital Revolution. Almost everyone's life has been revolutionized by developments in digital technology in the last twenty five years. Mobile devices and phones, email and the Internet are central in the day to day lives of every child and adult. This is a revolution that continues to develop with increasing momentum. It is almost impossible to keep up with it.

> "The internet is a tidal wave drowning those
> who do not learn to swim in its waves."
> Bill Gates, quoted in Digital Business, 1996.

Over the same period another revolution has been taking place that should have been making the same major changes to our lives as those brought about by mobile technologies and the Internet. Although it also has the potential to bring tremendous benefits to every adult and child in society, this revolution has made little impact on our day to day lives. Yet the effects of these discoveries should be like another 'tidal wave' that is no less powerful than the digital revolution. What is this revolution? It is a *Learning and Teaching Revolution*.

This series of books has been written to familiarize you with this revolution so that you can benefit from it and not be by-passed. I hope to do this by introducing you to some of the exciting discoveries about how the brain learns. In the light of this I also hope that you will be persuaded that to *learn about learning* is vitally important and that knowing how the brain learns is fundamental to successful, lifelong learning.

Even before you were born you were continually learning. It is what the brain was created to do and is what it does best. What a tragedy it is when someone concludes that he or she is 'no good' at learning as a result of school experiences or, even worse, disengages with learning. Our capacity to learn is one of the most exciting things about being created human. However, all too often, young people and adults have a *negative attitude* to learning. Past school experiences have convinced them they are inadequate and are not able to learn. In fact, education has 'turned them off' learning. They see learning as something *done to* them in a classroom, not *done by* them in the world. This is particularly damaging because

> **Your most valuable asset in learning
> is a positive attitude.**
> *Bobbi Deporter, Quantum Learning, 1992*

Everyone *needs to believe* that they can learn. I have emphasized that learning is critical for the changing world of work and has implications for the future of society as we anticipate living longer and having to adapt to the challenges of ageing. Before we consider how this relates to the world of work, let's return to the issue of ageing and mental decline. You may not be aware that dementia has replaced cancer as the number one health fear for people over sixty five. It is the greatest health challenge facing every society in the world—not only in the West. The risk of developing dementia will continue to increase for the present generation of young people and adults under fifty at present. Alzheimer's Research UK predicts that nearly one third of babies born in 2015 will develop dementia later in life. The number of people living into their eighties and nineties with dementia will pose unsustainable strains on every nation's health services.

> **Dementia is now the number one fear for over- 65s.**
> *Fingerprint Learning BrainFit Research*

In the absence of effective drug treatments, lifelong learning—literally from the cradle to grave—is the most effective way to prevent or delay dementia. It is also one of the best ways to sustain a better quality of life in older age. The motivation to learn and the satisfaction that comes from learning can be developed in childhood and youth. If this is nurtured throughout life it will contribute to a healthy brain in later years and be a crucial defence against mental decline. For this reason, ***lifelong learning has a vital medical application and not just an application to education and employment.*** If people are 'turned off' from learning at any stage of life there will be consequences in later life. So nothing could be more important than appreciating that everyone *needs to* learn 'for life' and that everyone *can* learn.

The importance of understanding how learning happens is relevant to many aspects of the world of work. One of these is in the role that business plays in the economy and particularly in the development of a wealth-creating 'enterprise culture'. Without this our society will not be able to afford the health costs associated with dementia or the education costs for the next generation of learners. A wealth-creating economy depends on one specific group of people—entrepreneurs. Many of these men and women, who have succeeded in the world of social or commercial enterprise, were turned off learning in school. Indeed, the ways in which the brains of many entrepreneurs learn are diametrically opposite to the ways in which formal education expects young people to learn and how it assesses and rewards their learning achievements. Despite their experiences in education they needed to be encouraged and convinced after leaving school that learning was indeed 'their thing'.

The brain is, above all, *the organ of learning*. The eye *sees*, the stomach *digests*, the ear *hears* and the brain *learns*. The brain is always learning and learning is what it excels at. The amazing discoveries about the brain in the last twenty five years should be revolutionising educational practice in the 21st century. Two important factors over this period of time have led to these discoveries.

The *first* is the massive investment in research into brain disease in the last decades of the 20th century.

The *second* is the extensive use of brain scanners in research in the 1990s. This technology enabled researchers to observe what was taking place in a living brain while they were experimenting. Before this they had been confined to dead, damaged or diseased brains for research.

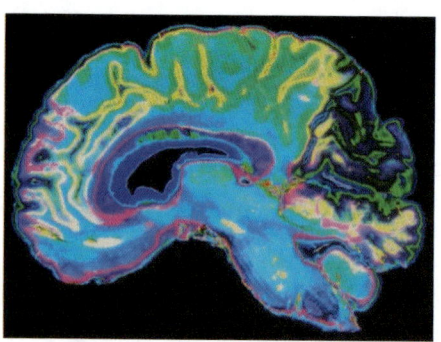

Brain scanning technology led to new discoveries about the brain as the organ of learning in the body. It was now possible to understand how the brain learns by observing it as it functioned. The implications for education were incalculable and were nothing short of revolutionary for every person in society. *So, whether you are a parent or a teacher, young or old, in business or an academic, let me welcome you to the Learning and Teaching Revolution!*

16

The entry point into this revolution involves answering one very important question—What is Education? Before we begin to look into how learning takes place in the brain I will first consider what education is. Over years of experience in teaching I have observed that people have various reactions to the word 'education'. What is your own reaction? For some it is a *positive* reaction—both emotionally and intellectually. For others the word has *negative* connotations associated with their experiences of school. So, what is education? I suggest it is *'transmitting and receiving information'*.

Richard Restak suggests that *information* is the unit of exchange *within* the brain and *between* brains. Information is what the brain 'trades in'. Your brain connects new information received through experience or instruction. It also connects information it *already possesses*, but had not connected before. This is an `Aha` moment.

Formal education involves the teacher, whose brain has already made connections about a subject, trying to make the same connections in the brain of the learner. If he or she succeeds in doing so, then learning has taken place. However, if they do not, then *teaching* taken place—but *not learning*. If that is the case, then what was the point of teaching? A teacher may have fulfilled the teaching requirement in terms of delivering the curriculum content, but if no learning took place it was wasted effort on the part of the teacher and student. It was an inefficient and ineffective exercise. The *teaching* objective may have been reached without reaching the more important *learning* objective.

Making these connections should be exciting and satisfying for children and adults. We have all seen the delight on an infant's face when he or she achieves a new skill, teaching us that, innately, learning should be fun! Learning is therefore about making connections between units of information – and making those connections stick! If the connections were not made in the learner's brain, teaching may have taken place, but learning has not. So, as I tell my own students,

Teaching **takes place in a classroom
but** *learning* **takes place in the brain.**

In other words, if the connections were not made in the brain, teaching may have taken place – but learning has not happened. Of course making connections stick involves **memory**, a vital function of the brain. We will deal with this in a later chapter.

One of the most exciting discoveries about the brain is that it is actually *'wired' to make connections*, through eighty six billion nerve cells or neurons with trillions of interconnections. Information is transmitted along these brain cells in tiny electrical signals. Each cell then transmits the information to connecting cells.

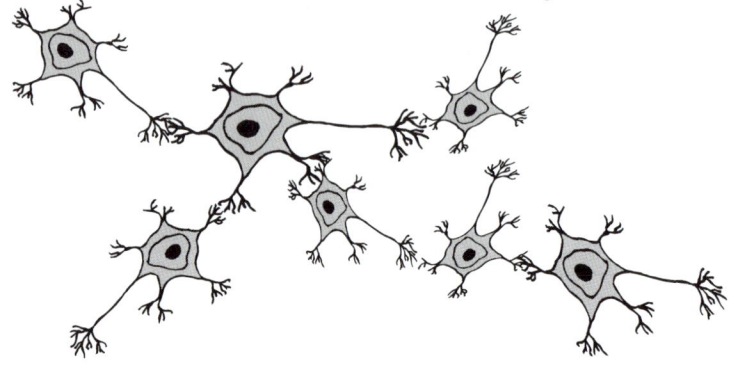

However, a further discovery about the brain and learning is that, although every brain is 'wired to learn', *not every brain is wired to learn in the same way.* The wiring of an individual's brain is the result of genetics and learning experiences i.e. nature and nurture.

The uniqueness of the wiring of each brain is amazing and has huge implications for teaching and learning. It is like a *learning fingerprint*!

> **"The individuality inherent in our brain networks makes that of fingerprints or facial features gross and simple by comparison."**
> *Roger Sperry, Nobel Prize Winner.*

Hence *Fingerprint* **Learning**!

The variety of ways in which the brain is wired to learn has been likened to the grain in wood. If you plane wood *with the grain* you will get a smooth action and the desired result. However, no matter how good the plane is, if you plane the wood *against the grain* the action is stiff and the result is rough and unsatisfactory.

When someone is taught or learns *with the grain* of his or her brain *learning will always take place*. It is what the brain does. However, if the same person is taught, or tries to learn, *against* the grain of the brain, learning takes much more effort and is often unsuccessful. The learner may even be discouraged about his or her ability to learn and disengage from formal learning altogether. You may have experienced this yourself. The example I have given about entrepreneurs illustrates this. Teaching approaches in formal education are usually in the opposite direction to the *grain* of an entrepreneurial brain.

Learning does not proceed in neat progressive steps. It is more helpful to think of learning as a process of completing a *cycle* of learning. In the **Learning Cycle** learners move from *what they want to learn* to *successful learning*.

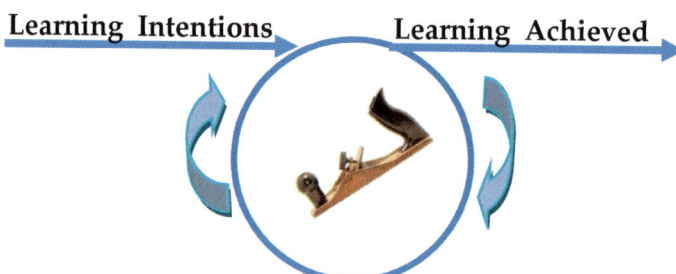

Success in learning involves *completing the Learning Cycle*. Whether someone completes the Learning Cycle or not, or *the rate* at which they progress through the Cycle, will depend on whether they are being taught—and are learning—*with* the grain of the brain or *against* it.

We have seen that
- education is transmitting information.
- information is transmitted through neuronal connections in the brain i.e. neuronal wiring.
- the brain is therefore wired for learning.
- not every brain is wired for learning in the same way i.e. each brain has an individual grain to it.
- effective learning takes place when we learn with the grain of the brain.
- teaching is most effective when it works with the grain of the learner's brain.

Some questions to consider before we move on.
Based on what we have covered so far, here are some questions you might like to consider. I hope you will be able to answer all of them when you have completed this book.
- Are you being taught but not learning?
- Were you expected to learn with or against the grain of your brain in your work or study?
- Do you have a child who is being taught, but is not learning?
- Whose problem is it if you or your children are not learning?
- Have you, as a parent, grandparent youth worker, or even a teacher or lecturer, ever considered yourself as a practitioner of learning?
- As a learning practitioner, what do you know about the organ of learning you are working with i.e. the brain?
- As a learning practitioner, do you know the grain of your own brain?

CHAPTER 2

Learning in Infancy and at Primary Level

We are going to start our exploration of what learning is about at the beginning of a child's life because an amazing amount of learning takes place in the earliest days, months and years of life—apart from any formal or structured education.

Because the brain starts to develop during pregnancy, *learning begins in the womb*. The interconnected 'wiring' of neurones (brain cells) takes place in the brain during the various stages of development. It is this 'wiring of the brain' that allows all normal development to take place.

Brain cells connect by transmitting information in tiny electrical signals and these signals travel from cell to cell through 'synapses'. These synapses increase in number in response to the stimulation the brain cell receives and make it possible for one cell to connect to up to 10,000 others. In this way information 'networks' begin to develop as information pathways in the brain connect information throughout the brain.

> **Within the next minute an average of 250,000 brain cells will have multiplied in each and every well-nourished growing foetus in the world.**
> Richard Restak, *Optimising Brain Fitness, The Great Courses.*

There is a huge increase in these synapses in infancy and early years. Also, during this period, there are special phases in which the brain of an infant or child is particularly responsive to developing interconnections.

For instance, information pathways for speech and vocabulary usually expand at specific times. This accounts for the astonishing ability of infants' brains to 'explode' in their willingness to try new words and make sentences. These special phases of neuronal development also make it possible to identify and look for specific milestones in child development which should match normal brain development.

At birth, the massive increase in sensory input to the brain leads to nothing short of a micro-explosion of brain activity. Sight, sounds, feeling, touch, emotion, early stages of memory and movement all involve the basic processes of learning and the wiring and re-wiring of the brain to respond to and absorb the information flooding into it. *The brain starts to connect information — in other words, to learn.*

For instance, it begins to receive sensory information in the *form of sounds* it hears people speaking. Later these sounds will be connected to other information to allow *speech*. The same information networks that store the sounds will connect the sounds to *specific symbols*, i.e. letters. Eventually the information network will be extended to link the sound to symbols in reading and later, movement, in writing. This building of information networks in the brain is what learning involves and is what the brain does best.

> **Children's work is their play.**
> **Children learn from everything they do.**
> Carolyn Hooper, New Zealand Play Centre Movement, 1992.

Children are born to *explore*. For instance, a new object is touched, held and manipulated by the hand. The object is lifted to the mouth. My granddaughter did this with my glasses when she first saw them. She grasped them with her hand and then put them to her lips. Her brain was making connections and she was learning! These sensory signals from the hand and lips and eyes are all sent to the brain to be interconnected to the existing networks.

The procedures are repeated again, the connections are reinforced—and *the child is learning*. Repeating movements or procedures lays down information pathways in the brain—like making paths though untrodden grass.

Exploring sometimes involves risks and it is important to recognise the difference between 'fire situations' and 'swing situations'. You don't take a risk with fire even if your child wants to explore it! We protect our children from situations that involve danger. However, some situations are 'swing' situations. There may be a potential danger in falling off a swing, but we encourage our children to learn how to try this. So, in some situations where the risk is not a danger, we need to push *our own boundaries* and not just our child's in letting him or her explore something new.

Formal 'education' is later going to 'interfere' with this natural process or, better still, *manage* it—hopefully in a constructive way. But learning *does not begin* with 'school' and formal education. In fact formal teaching can actually inhibit learning and prevent key learning pathways from forming.

For every infant and child a tremendous amount of learning, i.e. 'education', goes on during play. This is where the brain connections are being informally but effectively made. However, the brain is wired to develop through *active engagement* in what a child is doing. Watching a TV programme is essentially a passive activity and has very limited *learning value* in comparison to a parent conversing with the child about what is being watched. In Northern Ireland the Early Years Curriculum has been innovative in applying insights into how the brain learns to teaching infants.

Unfortunately this whole brain approach diminishes as a child progresses through school.

So for infants and children, the brain is stimulated to learn through engaging and exploring areas that are of direct interest to the child. Where you see an interest develop, physically or cognitively, you should encourage this and provide opportunities to expand the child's experiences and reinforce them through repetition. Seek to build vocabulary by talking and reading to your child, knowing the sounds are being stored in networks in the brain, ready to be connected to other networks when those special periods of development come along.

The more you link the more you learn.
Jeannette Vos, The Learning Revolution, 2001.

Children are also *naturally* creative and are keen to explore—which can involve risks. This is how children's brains learn and supervision should always facilitate this, not control or prevent it. Sir Ken Robinson has spoken about how schools deaden the innate creativity of children. Is it because his words ring so true in common sense terms that his talks are amongst the most popular in the TED Talks series? (TED talks by Sir Ken Robinson on 'How Schools Kill Creativity' on www.youtube.com). Parents should not expect formal education to take over the responsibility for their children's *learning*. They need to realise that learning is taking place all the time. As we will see in the next chapter, formal education may help or hinder your child's learning, but it is in *everyday learning* that their brains learn to process and respond to various emotions, relationships, crises, disagreements and disappointments.

It is in the experiences of daily life, as well as in nursery or school, that the grain of your child's brain is being 'planed' *with* or *against* the grain. Indeed it is in these early years that the grain of the brain can be most influenced.

Parents' Top Tips

Underline the tick if you *already* do this.
Circle the tick if you are *planning* to do so.

- ✓ I talk *to* my children and *with* my children as much as possible
- ✓ I listen to them and help them *build* their vocabulary.
- ✓ I help them to *explore* within safe boundaries.
- ✓ I recognise the difference between 'fire situations' and 'swing situations'.
- ✓ I realise that *play is learning* for my children and that their brains are 'making connections' as they play.

CHAPTER 3

Discovering the 'Grain of your Brain'.

If you judge a fish by its 'ability' to climb a tree it will spend its entire life believing it is stupid.
Albert Einstein

In the previous chapter we looked at how discoveries about the brain have revolutionised our understanding of learning, but have not yet brought about a revolution in teaching. We introduced the idea of the *grain of the brain* as a way of describing the differences in how our brains are 'wired to learn' through eighty six billion brain cells or neurones. In this chapter we will look at how you can discover the grain of your brain to enable you to engage in successful learning that is enjoyable and motivating. You will also discover how to recognize the grain of your colleagues', friends' and family's brains. If you are a parent or teacher you will be enabled to identify the grain of children's and students' brains.

One way of discovering the grain of the brain is by identifying what have been called '**Learning Styles**' or '**Learning Preferences**'. This terminology is unwelcome among those who favour traditional 'one size fits all' educational approaches. However, these terms have existed for a considerable time and are readily understood in the context of education. For our purposes we will consider that learning styles reveal, or provide a 'window' into, different 'grains' of the brain. These terms refer to the variety of ways in which the brain appears to take in and organise information. Different learning preferences reflect different *grains* of the brain.

While Learning Styles theory and practice have been identified for many years, discoveries about the brain in the last twenty-five years have added greater insights into what they mean and how they affect learning.

They can be a very useful tool in discovering why someone is not learning and not completing the Learning Cycle. They can also be used to find ways to learn more successfully and efficiently, i.e. *smarter* learning rather than just *more* learning. In this book we will

- look at some of the more well-known learning styles and apply them to different age groups in the contexts of education and work.
- help you identify your own learning style and the learning styles of others.
- show you how to use them to improve learning.

The question is not *how smart* people are but *how* they are smart.

One of the best known approaches to learning styles is the Multiple Intelligences Theory developed by Professor Howard Gardner (1983). Children learn early on to work out how smart or clever they are in comparison to others. Parents tend to do this as well. When we deliver the Fingerprint Learning workshops to schoolchildren we find that they can easily tell us how clever they think they are—or aren't. When we ask how Intelligence or Smartness is measured in schools, they always say 'Tests', 'Exams'. When they are asked which subjects are considered to be more 'intelligent' ones than others, English, Maths and Science are always mentioned first. In other words, schoolchildren of all ages tell us that being intelligent is measured in school by being good at exams in English, Maths and Science. This may be what their parents think as well, and reflects the hierarchy of subjects usually promoted by Government Education policy.

Proficiency in Drama, Dance, Music, Sport and other subjects are not considered by young people to be as highly valued in school as English, Maths and Science. There is a hierarchy of subjects to be good at if a child is to consider himself or herself intelligent.

This narrow, restricting and, I believe, damaging approach has been widely accepted in formal education for far too long and must be challenged. *The Multiple Intelligences Approach* provides such a challenge. In Fingerprint Learning we present this approach in eight ways of being smart, or **the eight Smartnesses.**

- **Word Smartness**
- **Seeing Smartness**
- **Music Smartness**
- **Body Smartness**
- **Nature Smartness**
- **People Smartness**
- **Self Smartness**
- **Number Smartness**

Although this approach has been around for decades and most teachers are aware of it, schools and education examination boards too readily ignore the potential it has to completely transform a learner's self-concept and his or her potential. In a curriculum that values individual learners, instead of a hierarchy of subjects with Maths, English and Science at the top, all eight Smartnesses are considered of equal value. Instead of a child asking, *"How smart am I?"* he or she is taught to ask, *"How am I smart"*? *Every child is smart* in many of the eight ways, and each Smartness is valued equally. On our training courses we find that when children learn to think of themselves in this way their self-esteem is boosted and they value themselves according to what they *can do*, not according to what they *can't do*. A favourite quote of my colleague and friend Joe Reid is that

'Success comes in Cans and not in Can'ts.'

If 'education' and teaching concentrates on what a child or young person *cannot* do it becomes 'deficit–focused'—as does the child, parent and teacher. But if, instead, the child's education focuses on what he or she *can* do, teaching and learning become a completely different experience for the child, parent and teacher.

This approach to 'Smartness' also helps children see and appreciate the abilities that other children have and to affirm these. Peer approval is a powerful asset in creating a learning culture or environment in a school. In schools where they have adopted a 'How am I smart' culture, children are recognized and rewarded for their Smartnesses, *as well as* ability in exams and tests. One Primary school in Belfast adopted this approach throughout the entire school. On entering the school children and parents are met by a wall display of children who have been recognized for various Smartnesses. A focus is placed on this in one of the weekly school assemblies and the children learn that it is not just Literacy and Numeracy that are rewarded, but all eight Smartnesses.

The following chart has a sample of characteristics for each of the eight Smartnesses drawn from a variety of Multiple Intelligence assessments. We have chosen to include some characteristics that would frequently be considered as 'problem behaviour' in a child. In other words, these are behaviours to be corrected—'deficits'! However, for the parent and teacher who understands Smartnesses, these features can be pointers to the 'grain' of a child's brain and be turned to positive uses in teaching and training a child. For instance,

A pupil who talks too much could be Word Smart! Word Smartness is not only skill at using words in reading or writing but in the use of words and vocabulary.

Someone who is dyslexic might have difficulty with reading and writing, but still be Word Smart in the use of words.

A Seeing Smart child may get into trouble for doodling in class or daydreaming.

What about a pupil who works better when there is some rhythm in the background, for instance, tapping a pen or pencil as he or she works?

Or what about a child who gets into trouble for being restless and not sitting in one place?

A Self Smart student may be happier to work alone rather than join in with others and so could appear to be unsociable.

A People Smart child may prefer to work in a team, or in pairs with friends.

Number Smartness is also Logical Smartness. Recognising right and wrong in Maths is vital and a child may display this in pointing out mistakes, or standing his or her ground in arguing against someone they consider to be mistaken.

As you read these characteristics, see if you can recognise children or adults you know who are strong in any of these Smartnesses. Can you see them in yourself, that is—*How are you smart?*

SMARTNESSES

Word Smart
- Good with words in speaking or writing and reading.
- Gets into trouble for talking too much.
- Enjoys discussing things.

Seeing Smart
- Likes to take things apart and put them together again.
- Good at jigsaws, 'Where's Wally', Spot the difference.
- Day dreams.

Music Smart
- Hums, sings, whistles or taps fingers to music.
- Drums with fingers on a table.
- Dances and moves to music.

Body Smart
- Good at copying physical movements.
- Finds it hard to sit still for long periods.
- Good at dance, drama or sport.

Nature Smart
- Knows the names of animals, flowers, constellations etc..
- Likes to get close to animals or work in a garden.
- Has a pet or would like to have a pet.

People Smart
- Senses when someone is down and wants to cheer them up.
- Likes to be with other children/people.
- Careful not to say hurtful things.

Self Smart
- Needs to be alone and not always with others.
- Content to play/work on his or her own.
- Gets into trouble for not joining in.

Number Smart
- Good with numbers.
- Can calculate time easily.
- Spots mistakes readily.

These Smartnesses are not fixed but can be developed, or even lost, in a child. For instance, we have found that many children are Nature Smart at Primary level, but when they become teenagers lose that Smartness. This is especially true with boys. We came across an exception to this when we were delivering Fingerprint Workshops in a school in Belfast. Among the Year 10 boys there was an unusually high number of Nature Smart boys. We discovered that one of the most popular clubs in the school was the weekly lunchtime Pets Club, when teachers and guests brought animals into the school! In this way, the Nature Smartness of the Primary school years had been nurtured in the boys, rather than being lost. This is exciting, because it means that from the earliest years it is possible to develop weaker and stronger Smartnesses in a child if we have a vision to do so.

The Smartnesses can help you recognise innate abilities in the youngest child. For instance,
- swaying to music in a Music Smart child; an interest in animals in a Nature Smart child.
- restlessness in a Body Smart child.
- ability to take things apart and put them together in a Seeing Smart child e.g. Lego.

Children should be praised for these as they grow up, even if school does not reward them – especially if it does not do so! The Smartnesses they are weaker in should also be encouraged and developed specifically, especially through play.

Smartness and Careers

Potential careers and jobs can be identified through Smartnesses. In working with young people we have found that they can easily suggest careers that go with each Smartness. This can raise aspirations and ambitions for children who come from an educationally weak background, or have not been 'academically' strong themselves. The following chart gives examples most frequently suggested to us by young people for four of the Smartnesses. Try it yourself for other Smartnesses.

> **Music Smart jobs**
> Singer, dancer, fitness instructor, musician, music teacher, songwriter, DJ, sound recording engineer.
>
> **Body Smart jobs**
> Armed forces, police, sports, fitness instructor, dancer, actor, PE teacher.
>
> **People Smart jobs**
> Counsellor, youth worker, social worker, minister or priest, teacher, nurse, doctor, psychologist, nursery school assistant.
>
> **Self Smart jobs**
> Singer, poet, artist, counsellor, psychologist, photographer, researcher, story writer/author.

A good time to introduce this is in the induction week of the first year of Post-primary school. We have found this to be well-received by pupils, who seem to grasp the approach readily and are eager to suggest jobs and careers that correspond to each Smartness. This can completely change a boy's or girl's view of himself or herself as a learner, whether the child got a poor grade in the Transfer Test or not. This approach encourages a child to think *'How am I smart?'* instead of 'How smart am I?' and, at twelve years of age, to begin to aspire to a career path based on personal Smartnesses. In this way Career advice begins at induction and ambition can be linked to achieving in subjects that will help to realise personal goals. The benefits of this approach can be optimised by asking a pupil to do personal research into self-selected careers. Once again the focus shifts from what the pupil *can't do*—pass the Transfer test for a place in Grammar school—to what he or she *can do* and could do in the future in terms of work. Some Primary schools in Belfast have introduced this in their P7 classes to help pupils appreciate their Smartnesses and prompt them to think about future jobs and careers as they prepare to leave Primary school and enter Post-primary education.

The career selection a student makes in the first year of Post-primary education may change as the pupil progresses through school, but by the time of GCSEs or A levels selections he will have been linking career choices to personal Smartnesses for three to five years.

I was speaking about the Smartnesses at a Parents' Evening in one school. During the refreshments afterwards I was thrilled when a student, with a big smile on his face, told me he was 'going to be a dog warden' because 'I am Nature Smart.' The school had awakened this motivation in him—and had even encouraged the confidence he needed to tell a complete stranger *how* he was smart. This approach to careers is an excellent way to motivate students and make the job of teachers easier.

The 3 As: Aspiration, Achievement, Access.
Solving the problem of educational under-achievement (the 'deficit' focus again!) has received considerable publicity in Northern Ireland in recent years and is a common problem in socially disadvantaged communities throughout the world. This approach to Smartnesses could be a transformative and inexpensive part of the solution, with valuable social benefits. Understanding and valuing people for their Smartnesses can have

an impact on parents' self-esteem as well as on that of their children. In Fingerprint Learning programmes for hundreds of students and parents over the last nine years we are constantly asked why this is not taught and practised in all Primary and Post-primary schools. Teenagers who are not in Education, Employment or Training—sometime referred to as 'NEETS'— have frequently told us, during Fingerprint Learning Workshops, that if this approach had been taken in school they would not be in a NEETS 'Programme' at all. In our experience this approach brings positive results because it raises **Aspiration** through demonstrating what someone *can do now* and *could do* in terms of a future career. Since lack of aspiration may be endemic in a family or a whole community for any combination of educational, social, or economic reasons, *raising aspiration* is a key to raising **Achievement.** The outcome of this is more likely to be **Access** to further education, training opportunities and employment.

Aspiration ⟹ **Achievement** ⟹ **Access**

Why *start* with trying to raise **Achievement**? Putting pressure young people (and teachers) to work harder on educational `deficits` to achieve better results has not worked in the past.

Fingerprint Learning has had the privilege of training staff, students and parents in this Learning Styles approac and I believe it has the potential to impact whole communities in which schools are located. Parents who 'under-achieved' in their own education can recognize their own Smartnesses as well as those of their children. The impact of this may mean that they are no longer on the `back foot` regarding their children's education. Their own sense of educational inadequacy—growing up conscious of what they couldn't do and how smart they are not—may have caused them to be dis-engaged in their children's education. But grasping the simple insights of the eight Smartness and asking `How am I smart?` or *'How is my child smart?`* transforms their view of themselves and their ability to help their children.

Parent-teacher meetings can focus not only on Numeracy and Literacy at Primary level or academic achievement at Post-primary level, but on the Smartnesses of each child. Teachers and parents are able to communicate on a broader range of a pupil's abilities and aspirations.

The Fingerprint Learning Parents' Workshops also provide parents with a toolkit of practical ways to use their children's Smartnesses to learn more effectively and more efficiently, i.e. *Smarter* learning and not just more pressure to learn.

The same toolkit is also provided for teachers so that they can not only identify and utilize the stronger Smartnesses of a pupil in developing study skills and learning techniques, but show them how to use stronger Smartnesses to assist in using their weaker Smartnesses.

Community-focused Government funding has made it possible to deliver programmes on Smartnesses in disadvantaged communities in Northern Ireland since 2007. The lives and futures of hundreds of people have been transformed. Some of their stories can be seen in the short video at www.fingerprintlearning.com.

Health and Wellbeing are known to be linked to educational aspiration and achievement. Through Public Health funding Fingerprint Learning has helped adults who 'failed' at school, leaving with few or no qualifications, to raise their aspirations and go on to access further training or education for a career. One of the first ladies to go through a Smartnesses workshop in 2007 had left school with no qualifications. When her Smartnesses were identified she gained enough confidence and self-worth to attempt and pass GCSEs, and completed a Psychology degree at University! She is a good example of how raising *Aspiration* led to *Achievement* and on to *Access* to Higher Education.

We have found that when young people are introduced to the Smartnesses, even at Primary school, it not only raises their own aspirations, but helps them value the Smartnesses of others. In one Primary school the teacher taught the Smartnesses to the children and then they helped one another recognize *how they were smart*. The children could see this in each other and it was then put on a wall display in the form of a class `mindmap` and attention drawn to it throughout the year. This was very affirming for every child in the class. In encouraging teamwork, it was also an excellent way to help children cooperate with the Smartnesses of others in completing a task or project using their various Smartnesses to make a contribution.

In our Fingerprint Learning workshops for retired people we try to help them recognise these Smartnesses in their grandchildren and use them to encourage them. This can mean a lot to a child who is struggling with self-esteem or finding school challenging, especially when it comes from someone they respect and who loves them—and who does not attend parent teacher interviews!

When a grandparent tells a child who is struggling with schoolwork that she is People Smart when she has shown care and sensitivity to others, this can really boost his or her confidence.

A boy who has been categorised as having 'special educational needs' will be helped enormously when he is told 'You are (Nature) Smart'. The impact is even greater when the child himself says, '*I am* (Nature) Smart'!

This is a practical example of reversing the emphasis from deficit-focused education to potential-focused education—from what the child *cannot do* to what he or she *can do!* After Smartness workshops there is no greater satisfaction than hearing a child or young person say, **"*I am smart*,"** perhaps for the first time in his or her life!

We have met young people in our workshops who had been told in school, or by parents, that they were stupid or dumb or a waste of a Grammar school place, or just a `waste of space'! The impact of this on a student's learning is immeasurable.

When a young man completed the Smartnesses workshop as part of a NEETS training programme, he said *'If my teachers had known this at school I would have done so much better. I think every teacher at Primary and Secondary School should do this programme.'*

As I have already mentioned, I find that when parents understand these eight Smartnesses they see themselves and their children differently. It boosted *their own self-esteem* and encouraged them to engage more with their children's education and schooling. This is especially so where the parent did not achieve academically and feels inadequate in the area of education.

One mother who attended the workshop recognised that her son was not very Word Smart but was very Nature Smart with a keen interest in birds. He was anxious about a word-based homework. He had been given homework to write a list of words beginning with each letter of the alphabet. His mother saw the solution in his Nature Smartness. She suggested he write *a list of birds beginning with each letter of the alphabet.* He succeeded—and enjoyed it. His mother had used what she had learnt about Smartnesses to engage with his homework herself.

One Primary school teacher shared in a Smartness workshop how he was Body Smart, but had been weak in Number Smartness in school until he had a teacher who took the class into the gym to teach Maths through movement. He learnt his Maths through his Body Smartness. This is an example of how a stronger Smartness can be used to help a weaker Smartness. Of course much of this is common sense and good teaching has always employed this approach without realising *why* it works.

We are all familiar with how Music Smartness is used to teach the alphabet along to a tune – a,b,c,d,e,f,g etc. The old method of teaching tables to a *rhythm*—'two ones are two, two two's are four' etc.—helped a Music Smart child grasp their tables more easily. This is using the grain of the brain to complete the Learning Cycle.

Checklist for Top Tips

You might like to respond to these Checklist questions with a Y for yes and an N for no.

Identify which of the eight Smartnesses are stronger for you.

Have these influenced your choices in work or leisure?   Y or N
Were your Smartnesses recognised/rewarded in school?   Y or N
Would it have made a difference if they had been?   Y or N
Now look at your children or grandchildren, nieces or nephews.
Can you see *how* they are smart?   Y or N
Are these Smartnesses being rewarded in school?   Y or N

And now the Top Tips

Underline the tick if this statement is true for you already.
Circle the tick if you are intending to put this into practice.

- ✓ Talk to your children about 'How they are smart' and begin to link this to possible jobs of people they know e.g. Sports people who are Body Smart, Musicians who are Music Smart.
- ✓ When reading stories, point out how people or animals are smart in different ways.
- ✓ Encourage children you already know to develop all eight Smartnesses as much as possible.

CHAPTER 4

Smarter Learning for *Better* Learning

Learning is most effective when it is fun.
Peter Kline, The Everyday Genius, 1997.

Do you believe this?
Do you think your children do?
It is how learning *began* for all of us—before we even knew that we *were* learning!

This was when we were learning *most* and at the *fastest rate* we ever would in our lives.

In this chapter we will suggest practical ways you can use the eight Smartnesses to help children learn in 'Smarter' ways that will:

- match the grain of their brains—not mismatch it.
- help them complete the Learning Cycle.
- make learning fun.

Here are some simple suggestions to get you and your children started.

Word Smart

- Look for **KEYWORDS** in text i.e. select *the main words* in a handout or book.
- Write these on a sheet of paper and on the same page, link other important words in the text to the Keywords in a spidergram or in a list underneath the Keyword.
- Let them record what they are learning on a digital recorder and then listen to it.

Seeing Smart

- Use *colour highlighters* to highlight text or *coloured pens* to make notes.
- Write out the KEYWORDS as in Word Smartness, but with coloured pens.
- Find images they can look at that are linked to the text they are reading, e.g. pictures, computer images, DVDs.
- Find diagrams they can copy and revise from.
- Try using spidergrams and brain-branch diagrams (or 'mindmaps') to make notes or revise information they need to learn. Use these to plan essays or projects before they start to write.
- Always re-write work in the *same position on the page* when they are learning it.

Music Smart

- Use their musical Smartness to remember information, e.g. to learn a list of words or names put the lists of words to tunes of songs they already know.
- Put the information they are learning into a 'rap'.
- Tapping their leg or an object with one hand to a rhythm as they recite information they are trying to remember.

Body Smart

- When they are learning, move to different locations in the house or different parts of a room as they study. They will find they concentrate more than by staying in one place for too long.
- Going outdoors and learning from their notes as they walk about. Going over the same information as they pass certain houses or landmarks on their walk.

Nature Smart

- Link information they are learning to something in nature that already interests them. For instance, make headings that are associated with certain animals, or star constellations, or planets.
- Review information outdoors, using the same locations to review the same topics.

People Smart

- Encourage them to do homework and study with friends or revise and review work with friends – provided they are doing the work!
- Make going out with friends a *reward for* when they complete the work they have to do.

Self Smart

- They will do better at work that has a personal meaning for them and that they can do alone.
- They will also be motivated to work better with self-assessment and personal target-setting.

Number Smartness

- Work that involves logical thinking, planning ahead, spotting mistakes and mental calculations will suit them.
- They can sometimes be argumentative if they spot inconsistencies or mistakes.

Above all, if their stronger Smartnesses are not being recognised and rewarded in school, be sure to give them plenty of recognition and reward at home. Help them recognise other people who share their Smartnesses. That Smartness may be a clue to their future career path. Draw children's attention to people who are in a career path—celebrities or people they know or admire—and ask if they can spot how these people are smart.

- Was Wayne Rooney Body Smart in school?
- Was Ed Sherrin Music Smart in school?
- Were Ant and Dec People Smart in school?
- Was Bear Grylls Nature Smart in school?

In the *Fingerprint Learning Workshops for Parents* we have also found an enthusiastic response when parents recognised not only their children's Smartnesses, but their own.

Among our most satisfying whole-brained workshops have been those for parents of children on the Autistic Spectrum as well parents of children with Dyslexia. Their children have been 'labelled' according to a specific learning 'deficit' that emphasises what they *can't* do. When parents learned to *identify how their children were smart,* it transformed their own view of their children and gave them tools to affirm their children and build their self-confidence.

Remember, *"Success comes in Cans and not in Can'ts."*

The last word in this chapter goes to the originator of Multiple Intelligences Theory;

> **A uniform way of teaching and testing**
> **is patently unsatisfactory**
> **when everyone is so different.**
> *Professor Howard Gardner.*

This is common sense, isn't it?

CHAPTER 5

21st Century Education for 21st Century Learners

The world our kids are going to live in is changing four times faster than our schools.
Dr. Willard Daggett, International Centre for Leadership and Education, 1992.

Research into how learning takes place in the brain falls into the realm of what is known as Neuroscience. In the following chapters I will introduce you to discoveries about the brain that have increased our knowledge of what learning is about. In other words, insights from studies in Neuroscience have led to a better understanding of the factors that influence effective learning and teaching. This is what lies behind this statement that education should be where

the Science of learning meets the Art of teaching.
Beverley Park, Canadian Education Association, 2006

I have already suggested that these discoveries should have had a revolutionary effect on teaching, but this revolution has still to reach most classrooms. Of course, there are exceptions, but by and large, so much educational practice and teacher training is still based on 20th century models which have not been upgraded to the 21st century. It is so encouraging when schools engage with the learning revolution, but so many more could be benefit from getting involved. In the 21st century our schools, colleges, universities and businesses need to respond to this revolution so that learners can be brought up to speed in a world changing even more rapidly than when the statement that opened this chapter was made in 1992. This is especially so in the light of this insightful statement from the *Connected Classroom* 2007.

We are currently preparing students for jobs that don't exist, using technologies that haven't been invented, in order to solve problems we don't know are problems yet.

This was in 2007! In the 21st century we have sufficient knowledge about how the brain learns to educate in ways that can equip all learners for this exciting and challenging situation.

So far I have introduced you to some basic aspects of how the brain learns and to Multiple Intelligences—one of the better known Learning Style approaches. Before we move on I would like you to reflect on how your own learning style has influenced you while you have been reading the first four chapters.

Have you found any of these features helpful?
- **Highlighted text in colour**
- **Bullet points**
- **Images and pictures**
- **Stories and examples**

If so, this tells you about the grain of your brain and how it is 'wired' to learn! On the other hand, if any of these 'put you off' as you read, this also reveals the grain of your brain!

Whether you read this book
- **from start to finish**
- **from the back to the start**
- **dipping in to different sections**

is a reflection of the 'grain of your brain' and your personal learning style.

I outlined three objectives in the Introduction. These were to
- *inform and enthuse* you about the exciting discoveries about how the brain learns.
- *motivate* you to get involved in *lifelong learning* and to engage yourself and your children or pupils in this process.
- *apply* discoveries about learning to improve your own quality of life and also help you and your children and pupils become more successful learners.

I hope that what you have already read has started to fulfil these objectives and that the following chapters will continue to do so.

As you read on you will gain insights into your own learning style—your personal learning *fingerprint*—that will enrich your understanding of yourself as a learner and as a person, as well as equip you to help others to learn better. However, before we proceed to do this, it important to deal with one excuse sometimes given for not engaging in the learning revolution that we have been considering. In some quarters the application of discoveries about the brain to teaching and learning has been described as 'Neuro-nonsense' or 'Neuro-myths'. Sometimes this has been a response to exaggerated claims being made for the application of neuroscience to learning. In other cases it has been used to undermine the abundance of pragmatic evidence about how our brains are individually wired for learning.

The fiercest critics of Multiple Intelligences in education are frequently individuals whose smartnesses fit in with those that have been traditionally valued, for instance, Word smartness in reading and writing and Number smartness. Their own learning style was rewarded in school and they all too easily dismiss those who did not conform in the classroom as trouble-makers who simply did not try hard enough. People who label non-traditional approaches as 'Neuro-nonsense' or 'Neuro-myths' also tend to espouse a more dogmatic black and white world view which is unable to empathise with those who demonstrate alternative inclinations in learning. Because they are often attracted to the detached world of academia, they may also focus so much on publishing research based on 'experimentally proven facts' that they are blind to the complex reality of how human beings think and behave. It may be a case of 'not seeing the wood for the trees.' After reading this book you can judge for yourself whether the insights into how the brain learns should be dismissed as Neuro-nonsense or valued as important contributions to educational achievement and fulfilment for learners in all age groups.

In the following chapter we will take up the claim that neuro-science has little to offer in learning and teaching today.

CHAPTER 6

Fear, Failure—and Fun!

In the next two chapters I will explain some of the most significant applications of neuroscience to improve teaching and learning practice. Although it involves *neuro*science it is not *rocket* science! In fact, much of it is obvious once it is pointed out. We have found that young people, including NEETS (Adolescents Not in Education, Employment or Training), not only understand what this chapter explains, but respond by saying 'That's me! I am like that!'. We will look first at *the response of the brain to threat* and in the following chapter we will consider *the adolescent brain*.

The response of the brain to threat

The brain is 'wired' to respond *instantly and spontaneously* to anything that is perceived to be a threat. We have all experienced this in some way, but may not have understood how it works. A little neuroscience is necessary to understand this.

The upper part of the spinal cord, where it joins the brain, is called the 'Brain Stem'—because the brain is supported by it like a flower on a stem.

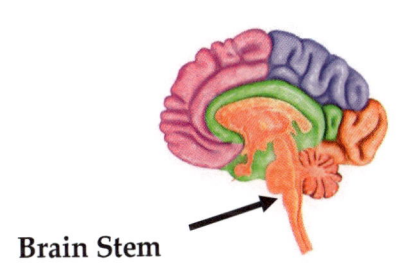

Brain Stem

The Brain Stem is where the *survival instinct* is located in the brain. When a special part of the brain (the Amygdala) is triggered, there is an instantaneous reaction in the Brain Stem. The result is that you *immediately react* by doing whatever is needed to protect yourself and survive the threat.

We are all familiar with this response which keeps us alive in dangerous situations. For instance, if you are calmly walking across the road and a car suddenly drives towards you, you don't continue to walk on without interrupting your thought. You jump out of the way, or hurry your pace. This response is instantaneous. It is not the result of rational thought and reasoning. You react immediately. This response is indispensable for survival. However, it can also have undesired influences on our lives. *Irrational f*ears or imaginary threats such as fear of heights, flying, insects or balloons can prevent someone from engaging in normal activities.

Reactions in the Brain Stem can have a major impact on preventing learning taking place in the brain. The survival response over-rides reasoning and therefore impedes learning.

When the Brain Stem is activated and 'kicks in' the higher reasoning and learning centres of the brain are suppressed. The Brain Stem over-rides them and the survival response dominates over 'reason'.

In a Fingerprint Learning workshop for teachers, one participant shared her reaction to cats. If a cat was in her presence, or she suspected a cat was about, she was paralysed. She 'froze' until someone could reassure her there was no cat around. Another participant had the same reaction to balloons. On another occasion, someone with reputation for fearlessness, admitted that a mouse—even a dead mouse—would cause him to leave the room! In one workshop a participant was honest enough to admit to a fear of oranges!

These are not rational responses, but it is pointless trying to 'reason' someone out of them when they have kicked in. The *reasoning* centres in the brain have been suppressed by the *survival reaction* in the Brain Stem. This is a critical factor in learning. When the survival instinct of the Brain Stem is activated, learning is not taking place.

As a medical student I was taught that when I told a patient that he or she had cancer I should immediately arrange a second appointment. This was because instructions given after breaking this news would frequently not register with the patient after the shock of hearing the diagnosis. Once the fear had subsided a further appointment was needed to ensure that the patient heard and received important information properly—in other words, that the reasoning centres of his or her brain had made the appropriate connections.

In a child, teenager, or adult, this can determine whether learning actually takes place or not. If the learner feels threatened, for instance, by trouble or trauma at home—a sudden illness in the family, family breakdown or violence—the ability of the student to learn will be impeded. Any threat from other pupils, or fear of the teacher, can prevent learning.

I was explaining the impact of threat and stress on learning during a Fingerprint Workshop to teachers in a Primary school in Belfast. The school had been providing much needed social stability in an area of the city that had suffered serious disruption through the Troubles. During the workshop the staff pointed out that a very high level of threat existed *within the whole community* from which the pupils were drawn and this had affected not only the children but the parents as well.

Fear of failure is one of the most common threats to learning in education. Failure in the eyes of peers, or parents or in the student's own eyes can be a powerful trigger for the Amygdala and Brain Stem.

I was asked to help one boy with whom a teacher had lost her temper when he failed to read correctly. He was only five years old when this had happened and the experience created a fear of attending that teacher's classes every day for a whole year. By the time I tried to help him the 'wiring' of his brain for learning had been so seriously impeded that I was unable to undo the consequences, which permanently marred his development.

For the *self-talking* student who needs to dialogue internally to make learning connections, the fear that a teacher is going to put him or her on the spot to answer a question can prevent learning throughout an entire lesson.

All learning involves a challenge. However, if the challenge becomes a *threat*, learning is suspended. If a parent or teacher responds to a student's slowness to learn in a threatening way — perhaps due to impatience or frustration on the part of the adult — the learning parts of the brain shut down and the Brain Stem kicks in. *If a child is not learning this should always be considered.*

Parents of children on the Autistic Spectrum shared that their children live continually with the Amygdala and Brain Stem at a high level of alertness — much higher than in other children. Sounds and activity, especially in unfamiliar contexts, interfere with the cognitive function of the cortex so that learning is impeded.

Most of us are familiar with the four survival responses to threat.
- **Fight** — a self-defence reaction of aggression to a teacher. This can be either verbal or physical. It might be totally inappropriate behaviour but, at that moment for the student, it is a question of survival.
- **Flight** — how can the student escape the situation, for example, by school avoidance, or even avoiding eye contact with the teacher in the hope that you will not be singled out for a question.

- **Freeze**—when the student knows the information but cannot get access to it at the time, e.g. in an exam situation. The information has already been connected in the brain but cannot be accessed because the Amydala has been activated.
- **Flock**—when a perceived threat makes the student want to retreat to the 'group', where he or she feels secure. For an infant in nursery class, this can be home and family. For a teenager, it can be the peer group.

It is vital to remember that the response is *not rational*. The reasoning centres are impeded. If learning is to take place, then the *challenge* of learning needs to be maintained, but the *threat* must be identified and removed. Any response by the teacher that *minimizes* the fear, or makes it look ridiculous because it is not rational, will only increase the threat level. A reaction of impatience or anger in the teacher or parent will also aggravate the problem. The impact of threat and fear in the learning process illustrates how much learning and emotion are linked together.

- Positive emotions facilitate learning.
- Negative emotions prevent learning.

Learning pathways in the brain are affected by emotions such as fear and can be 'freed up' for effective learning by:
- maintaining the challenge but removing the threat.
- giving feedback (helpful information) on work done or answers given, not just a right/wrong response by a teacher or parent.
- teaching *how to fail*. Everyone fails as they learn something new, but failing is not failure. *Fear of failure* activates the brain stem and prevents learning. Fear of failure can prevent a learner even attempting a new challenge because this fear is already embedded in the brain as a threat.
- building up confidence with approval and by affirming success. This is a powerful incentive to attempt new learning.

These insights are important contributions of neuroscience to our understanding of teaching and learning. Far from being *neuro-nonsense*, they can provide invaluable tools for teachers and tutors who are working with students who are underachieving educationally. Understanding how the brain responds in these ways and knowing how to *recognise* and *respond* to this should be fundamental to all teacher training. Indeed it provides insight into the behaviours and reactions of whole communities in which children live when *perceived threats* to one community lead to 'survival reactions' that threaten another community.

Turning *perceived threats* into *challenges* has been a key to building cross-community cooperation in Northern Ireland. However, when fresh threats emerge, old reactions can 'kick in' as the Brain Stem is activated for survival, however irrational it may seem to outsiders. Economic arguments against violent social protests are futile when the *fight* response has been triggered due to a perceived threat to the identity of a community

There is another side to the coin of how emotional responses to threat impede learning. This is the importance of *fun* in learning. If threat and fear *impede* learning pathways in the brain, enjoyment and fun in learning can 'free up' those pathways. Even as adults, we all learn better when we enjoy what we are learning about, or when we like the person teaching us. This is true for every child and student too. When information is taught in enjoyable ways the brain 'digests' it better.

Learning that is enjoyed does not even seem like learning. All learning involves challenge, but there are ways of making the challenge more fun during the process. If you want a child to learn, introduce as much fun as possible. It is like oxygen to the brain while it is exercising itself to make connections.

Time for another Checklist
Here is a Checklist for you to consider. You might like to respond to these questions with a Y for yes and an N for no.
Can you identify any threats in your life that cause irrational fears? Y or N
Can you recognise when this got in the way of functioning normally in situations? Y or N
Did you feel embarrassed when people made you feel foolish about this? Y or N
Can you identify how threats and fear are at work in the learning of your children? Y or N
Have these been handled sensitively by you or others? Y or N

And now for the Top Tips
Underline the tick if this statement is true for you already.
Circle the tick if you are intending to put this into practice.

- ✓ Talk with your child about how he or she feels when the threat kicks in.
- ✓ Discuss this with the child's teachers and discover how it is being handled in school.
- ✓ Remove the threat and maintain the challenge by devising strategies to help deal with the threat when it arises or to anticipate it.
- ✓ Be patient and *non-threatening* in how you address this with your child and seek to be understanding and supportive rather than pressurising them to perform. It may require a lot of time and patience to progress towards a resolution.
- ✓ Explain what is happening in the brain to provide a language with which they can communicate about their fears and can help them understand what is going on. For a young person it is important to communicate that there is nothing 'wrong' with them. Lots of people have irrational responses to perceived threats and fears.

CHAPTER 7

The Adolescent Brain

Changes in the brain during adolescence is another example of how neuroscience is relevant to good teaching and learning.

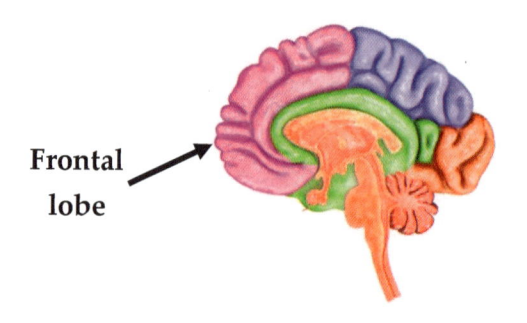

Frontal lobe

The **Frontal lobes** of the brain, and especially the area called the pre-frontal cortex, have been called the *Executive Centre* of the brain. The pre-frontal cortex is highly developed in human beings and is involved in

- making decisions.
- planning ahead.
- considering the consequences of our actions.
- determining what is appropriate or inappropriate behaviour.
- creativity.

This is where we are 'wired' to delay reward or gratification for a greater objective or goal.

For instance 'potty training' involves re-wiring the pre-frontal cortex of a child. Previously `pooing` or `doing a wee` in a nappy was *appropriate*. (Some parents are even particular about the appropriate terms to use for these bodily functions!) Now it is *inappropriate*. Strategies involving rewards and encouragements, rebukes and punishments may be set in place until the frontal lobes are re-wired for what is now appropriate i.e. using the toilet.

Consider another example. We are not born *knowing how to queue*—unless you are a second twin—yet our frontal lobes have been wired to look for the queue whenever we enter bank. If you were to walk up to the cashier out of turn there would be an instant reaction from others—so you join the queue. This is the appropriate behaviour and the frontal lobes have been wired for this. Children are taught to queue and take their turn at an early stage of their school experience. It is an important part of social learning. Their instinct is to reach and take what they want when they want it. Indeed, *if an infant did not do this* parents and health workers would be worried about a lack of development. But in Nursery school this is no longer appropriate. So the learning process regarding what is appropriate behaviour in waiting your turn is wired into their brain in the classroom.

Teachers can find it challenging to alter a child's behaviour in this way, especially when it involves learning what is appropriate or inappropriate. For instance, certain language and vocabulary may be appropriate in the home but be considered unacceptable or obscene in school. This can be confusing for the child whose brain is in the process of being wired under conflicting influences.

The same goes for certain kinds of behaviour. If aggressive behaviour, or anger, is modelled as appropriate at home, then there will be major challenges for a child in school.

We saw the relevance of reactions in the brainstem and survival, and how this can apply for whole communities. The same is true in the wiring of the frontal lobes. What is considered as appropriate behaviour in one section of the community may be considered completely inappropriate in another. The wiring of the frontal lobes has been shaped by the community view of what is or is not appropriate. This has a crucial application in adolescence which we know can be a difficult time of life for teenagers as well as for the adults in their lives. In puberty, powerful new impulses are released that the frontal lobes have to integrate into what is appropriate and inappropriate behaviour. Completely new desires and impulses that crave for immediate gratification are released in the adolescent. There has been no *preparatory learning* to wire the brain for these—it just starts to happen.

This cannot be taught theoretically in a classroom. It can only be learnt as the adolescent experiences it.

Adolescence involves complex combinations of new demands that have to be integrated by the frontal lobes. These include the need for approval and acceptance by a peer group, the accessibility of drugs, alcohol, online gambling, tobacco, together with sexual stimulation and gratification. This mixture can be overwhelming for the frontal lobes as they are forced to establish completely new connections and networks between neurones. What is appropriate or inappropriate *now*? Why should I delay gratification now for the sake of longer term goals?

The *collapse of a moral consensus* in society makes this even harder for adolescents. There has probably never been a more difficult time to be a teenager—for the adolescent, parents and teachers. The difficulty is increased by the fact that adults frequently expect adolescents to behave in adult ways. The recent popularity of *Fifty Shades of Grey* as mainsteam entertainment—the book and film made extraordinary sales—is a powerful example of how frightening this can be when we consider adolescents. The storyline is not about love or even sex, but about manipulation, control and submission. If actions considered previously as sexual perversion or deviation and completely inappropriate are now considered appropriate, what is going to happen to the wiring of our young people's brains—or our own. These kinds of books and films are re-wiring the brains of whole societies—and perhaps a civilisation.

Another example involves the distinction between what is *public* and *private*. Most people over 30 years of age grew up when there was a clear distinction between public and private life. The society and culture we grew up in set the 'default position' in the frontal lobes that was sensitive to what was appropriate for a private context or a public context.

Today the media, and especially social media, has not only blurred the distinction but has removed it completely. Teenagers and children are growing up in a culture where everything private is public, from what they ate for breakfast to what their girlfriends look like naked. This has massive implications for education going forward. How can we educate the frontal lobes to be wired to make *appropriate* responses if there is no longer any common agreement about what is appropriate—even among adults whose frontal lobes have matured?

The frontal lobes of the adolescent brain have a lot to cope with, *especially since they are still developing their 'wiring' until the late teenage years.* Indeed recent research suggests that the frontal lobes are still maturing even later than at nineteen years of age. This means that teaching and training teenagers is a process that requires skill and patience. It calls for a new appreciation of how challenging teaching is going to become for all learning practitioners, at home or in school. It also calls for an understanding of the difficulties that young people in education are facing and will increasingly face in the future. It is not only the *extent* of change that is alarming but the *speed* with which it is happening.

These examples illustrate why an understanding of the brain should be fundamental for every practitioner of teaching and learning—including parents. This has a particular application when we encounter what seems like behavior that is 'out of character'. One teacher shared with me how her usually level-headed, responsible 15 year old nephew took his parents' car one evening, collected his friends and drove them around Belfast. Fortunately he returned home safely, but if neighbours had not observed this, his parents would never have known. This was completely *inappropriate* behaviour in a normally 'sensible' adolescent boy!

The wiring of the frontal lobes is integrated into rewards systems and the feedback that comes from gratification through certain behaviour. Gratifying experiences or sensations reinforce the wiring for behaviours that are considered to be appropriate because they lead to the desired reward. The frontal lobe is wired for 'wins'. This has many applications in the lives of adolescents. For instance, the increased use of video games for entertainment as they are growing up 'wires' the brain for 'quick wins'. This works against future planning that delays the quick win for a long-term gain. Drugs, sex, gambling, all offer instant wins for the brain and this is why they are so frequently associated with addictive behaviours.

Getting adolescents to plan ahead and exercise self-control in order to achieve a long term reward is more challenging than ever. This is one reason why I encourage teachers and parents to build in frequent short term 'wins' into their teaching or training. The reward of a qualification at the end of a whole school year is not a quick win. Weekly and monthly rewards and benefits are ways of going *with the grain* of the adolescent brain and can lead to long term gains as well.

To fight *against this* is to fight the cultural context in which our young people have been growing up since childhood and will be a losing battle. Teaching in the 21st century involves persuading students how learning a particular subject or skill is going to bring them short-term benefits as well as long-term advantages.

This is an area where the application of neuroscience has so much to offer in education, but which most teachers are not being given access to. Could understanding how the frontal lobes determine behaviour and choices be a valuable tool for teachers and parents working with teenagers? Surely it must be fundamental to working effectively with the 'grain' of the adolescent brain?

Another Checklist
You might like to respond to this Checklist with a Y for yes and an N for no.
Can you remember any struggles you had as a teenager to determine what was appropriate and inappropriate thinking and behaviour? Y or N
Can you see where you have been re-wiring your child's frontal lobes to learn what is appropriate and inappropriate? Y or N
Do you realise how powerful *rewards* are in re-wiring the frontal lobes for changes in behaviour? Y or N
Can you recognise the struggles adolescent children or students are having as puberty releases new feelings and desires that call for gratification? Y or N

Now for the Top Tips
Underline the tick if this statement is true for you already.
Circle the tick if you are intending to put this into practice.

- ✓ Don't assume that someone who has conformed to what is appropriate as a child will automatically do so in adolescence.
- ✓ Keep your children talking when they reach adolescence and be sympathetic to the challenges their brains are facing.
- ✓ Give them frequent 'quick wins' to encourage them to move towards long term goals.

CHAPTER 8

Sensory Learning Preferences or VA(T)K

Information received by the brain is taken in by the senses. We could think of these as sensory 'pathways' which provide the information needed to construct neuronal networks in the brain. The Sensory Preference approach to Learning Styles is one of the most commonly known in school education and is often abbreviated to VAK, where
V = Visual (Sight)
A = Auditory (Hearing)
K = Kinaesthetic (Physical movement)
There are a number of variations in this approach to learning preferences and in Fingerprint Learning we favour the model of Dunn and Dunn (1993) which expands the abbreviation to VATK. In this model, Kinaesthetic learning is subdivided into Tactile and Kinaesthetic. The Dunn and Dunn model asub-divides these into nine possible sensory pathways. In this chapter I will introduce you to these and how we apply them in Fingerprint Learning.

Individuals have *preferences* and *non-preferences* in the senses they learn through and these influence the ease with which learning networks are formed in the brain. These sensory preferences are indications of the 'grain' of a person's brain i.e. they help you appreciate how you prefer to learn. They can inform a teacher or parent on how to teach *with* the grain of the learner's brain and not *against* it.

It is important to make clear from the outset that this approach to learning styles does not mean that a learner can say, 'I am a kinaesthetic learner and therefore should not be expected to learn in other ways.' In fact, most people can adapt to learning through different senses and it is very helpful if they do learn to do so. However, this is not true in all cases, and should not be an excuse for teachers failing to deliver information through as many of the

sensory pathways as possible, so that all learners are catered for.
Traditionally, education has emphasised delivering information through two sensory pathways in a very restricted sense. These are Visual—in terms of reading text, and Auditory—in terms of listening to a teacher speak. This has sometimes been summarised as the 'Chalk and Talk' approach. Although that would be considered outdated today, it is still true that formal education *overestimates* what can be learnt just through listening to a teacher speak and by reading text.

In this chapter I will give an overview of the various sensory preferences for taking information in and then suggest a few applications for each. It will be helpful if you can identify the Sensory Pathways that you prefer to learn through, as well as any that you find more challenging to learn through. This will help you, as a parent or teacher, understand the ways in which you expect others to learn as well. Sensory preferences are an indication of the grain of your brain. The preferences that correspond to the grain of your brain can make it harder to recognise the preferences of others. However if you are to adapt your *teaching style* to the *learning style* of the learner, it is important to understand what you automatically bring to the learning process, including any bias towards specific sensory preferences. This will allow you to see where you need to adapt and use other sensory pathways in teaching individuals who may not share your preferences. For instance, some learners have definite *non-preferences* for certain sensory pathways and struggle to learn information delivered in this way.

The following table summarises each of the sensory pathways under VATK.

Visual	Auditory	Tactile	Kinaesthetic
Reading text	Listening to monologue	Touching Handling Manipulating	Physical motion and external movement
Seeing diagrams, pictures, images	Listening to and taking part in discussion		Internal motion i.e. *e*-motion. Feeling good about a subject or a teacher
Internal vision i.e. imagination	Self-talk and internal dialogue		

Visual Sensory Pathways

Of the three kinds of visual sensory pathways, two are external and one is internal.

External
- Reading text in the form of textbooks, handouts, computer text or projected text.
- Information in the form of images, diagrams and graphics.

Internal
- Information received through the use of imagination.

Auditory Sensory Pathways
Of the three kinds of auditory sensory pathways, two are external and one is internal.

External
- Listening to a teacher speaking without the use of images.
- Listening through participating in discussion with others.

Internal
- Connecting information by listening to oneself in terms of self-dialogue or self-talk. Some learners need time and opportunity to talk over information within themselves.

Tactile
The hands and mouth are important receptors of sensory information. When you see infants investigating objects with their mouths you are observing an example of how they are taking information into their brains to form learning networks. Touch is another example. It is not merely a childish form of learning but an enduring sensory preference in many children, young people and adults. They learn better when they are able to handle and touch in the learning process. They can also get into trouble for fidgeting because they *need* to use their hands to learn best!

Kinaesthetic
This can also be considered in terms of External and Internal.

External Kinaesthetic
Information that is adapted to physical movement is more easily transferred into learning networks.

Internal Kinaesthetic
This involves the place of *emotion* rather than external *motion* in learning. When the learner feels positive about with the subject or the teacher, information is more easily absorbed into learning.

Learning with the grain is learning through the sensory pathways you prefer. How quickly a learner goes through the cycle—or how far through it he or she gets—is determined by how much he or she is *taught with the grain*.

In the case of sensory preferences, learning is facilitated when teaching is directed to a student's sensory preferences and not his or her *non-preferences*. For instance, I have frequently encountered learners who have a non-preference for learning through reading text. In some cases they have been CEOs in their own businesses who avoid reading documents and rely on their staff to provide the information in alternative ways. In a few cases this was due to dyslexia, but frequently it was due to a non-preference for taking information in through text.

As I have already indicated, most learners can adapt and should be encouraged to adapt to learning through sensory paths that are *not preferred*—but sometimes this can be so challenging that it discourages them and they dis-engage from learning through failure to complete the Learning Cycle. *Identical content* can be taught to children but the *degree of learning* will depend on which senses are engaged by the teacher or parent. If the same information was delivered through a sensory pathway appropriate for that learner, he or she would find completing the Learning Cycle much easier. Indeed, when a learner has become 'stuck' part way through the Learning Cycle a breakthrough can come by delivering the information through a different sensory pathway.

Successful teaching and learning is the result of knowing how to turn information into formats that correspond to a person's sensory preferences . For instance,
- turning *text* into *images* or *diagrams* e.g. computer icons.
- turning *information* into *movements* e.g. dance.
- developing *tactile* methods of engaging with the information, for instance, art or computer programmes.
- providing opportunity for discussion or internal dialogue.

The following Sensory Preference Indicator is a rough guide to identifying how you prefer to take information in. It may be useful in discovering how the learners you are teaching at home or in school prefer to take information in.

Sensory Learning Indicator

Tick your response under Yes or No. If you tick Yes, circle the corresponding option below.

	Visual (Seeing)	Yes	No
1A	I learn a lot by reading books or handouts or taking notes.		
1B	I learn more when I see images or pictures connected with information I am learning about e.g. in diagrams, video, DVD, TV, computer graphics.		
1C	<u>One or both</u> of these is true of me. • I learn more when I can use my imagination. • I daydream when I am not concentrating.		

I learn by best by   1A   1B   1C   (Circle your Yes options)

	Auditory (Listening)	Yes	No
2A	I learn a lot by listening to someone give a talk without needing to see pictures or diagrams.		
2B	I learn better when I am involved in discussion about a topic.		
2C	I talk into myself a lot, especially when solving a problem or doing something difficult.		

I learn best by   2A   2B   2C

	Tactile (Touching and Handling)	Yes	No
3	<u>One or both</u> of the following is true of me. • I like to use my hands to learn. • I fidget with pencils, pens or other objects when concentrating.		

I learn best by 3

	External Kinaesthetic (Movement)	Yes	No
4	I like to get up and move around rather than sit in one place for a long time.		

I learn best by 4

	Internal Kinaesthetic (Emotion)	Yes	No
5A	I learn better when I feel good about a subject.		
5B	I learn better when I feel good about a teacher or instructor.		

I learn best by   5A   5B

The numbers you have circled will tell you about the grain of your brain. They show how you learn best and what helps you to complete a Learning Cycle.

On the following page you will find some suggestions to match your sensory preferences.

You might like to try these out for yourself first and then try them for your children.

Practical Tips for Sensory Preferences

Auditory (Listening)

1A You will learn from courses that involve listening to talks or lectures, audio cassettes or CDs. Record yourself saying what you have to learn and remember, and then listen to it.

1B You will learn better when there is opportunity for discussion in a group, with a friend, or with the teacher or a parent.

1C You need time to think over what you are learning. You may not grasp it immediately or be able to answer questions straight away. This does not mean you are not smart. Teachers and parents who recognise a self-talking learner will avoid putting him or her on the spot or pressurising him or her to take part in discussions, otherwise the Amygdala will be activated and the Cortex will shut down! Fear of being put on the spot may prevent a self-talking pupil from learning throughout a lesson for this reason.

Visual (Seeing)

2A You will learn better from a textbook or from good handout notes.

2B You will learn better if you can watch a TV programme, video, DVD, or computer images about a subject. You will learn more from a textbook with pictures or diagrams, as well as by drawing diagrams about what you learn.

2C You will learn better when you can use your imagination and when a teacher tells stories or gives examples that you can imagine. You will remember information by including it in a story you make up, or turning the information into a drawing or painting.

Tactile (Touching and Handling)

3A You will learn better when the subject involves using your hands or practical skills. If you fidget when listening, use something that will not make a noise. Learning that involves using a computer keyboard is helpful. Make revision notes on small cards you can handle and turn over as you learn.

External Kinaesthetic (Physical Movement)

4 You will learn better when a subject involves physical movement, such as dancing, drama, outdoor activities. When you are learning, move from place to place in a room, or in a house every 20-30 minutes—or go outside and walk as you learn or revise!

Internal Kinaesthetic (E-motion)

5A When you have the chance to do so, choose subjects that really interest you.

5B If it is possible, choose a teacher or tutor you feel good about.

If you use these ways of learning you will be learning *with the grain* of your brain.

Checklist for Sensory Preferences

The checklist involves trying out the list of Sensory Preferences in the tables on yourself and on your children.

You might also like to respond to these questions with a Y for yes and an N for no.

Do you know what your sensory preferences are? Y or N

Do you have any non-preferences? Y or N

Can you recognise these in your children or the children you teach? Y or N

Have you ever discussed this with your child's teacher? Y or N

As a teacher do you try to include these different forms of communicating information by including every sensory pathway over a series of lessons? Y or N

CHAPTER 9

Two Brains in One

'Essentially, we have two brains in our head.'
Dr. Jeannette Norden,
Professor of Neurosciences at Vanderbilt University, 2007.

This chapter is about *Lateralisation,* or the difference in how the right and left hemispheres of the brain process information. Once you understand this you will gain a valuable and practical insight into yourself and others around you, as well as the children in your family or school class.

The brain is divided into *right* and a *left* hemispheres. They are connected and coordinated through a nerve pathway called the *Corpus Callosum.* Each hemisphere receives information from the senses but each hemisphere *processes the information* in different ways. This means each side is suited to *performing different tasks* and using different skills. For instance;

Left hemisphere	Right hemisphere
performing step-by-step tasks	performing intuitive and imaginative tasks
answering right or wrong questions	answering open-ended questions

Look at the following table and identify which characteristics are true for you. You might like to tick the box beside what is true of you most of the time and then add your 'score'.

Give yourself a 2, 1, or 0 for how strongly each category describes you.

73

(2 = mostly 1 = sometimes 0 = rarely)

	I focus on details and am careful to do things right.	I like to see the big picture and am less interested in details.	
	I like step by step instructions and doing things in order.	I don't complete tasks in a pre-set order but more randomly.	
	I rarely question reasons, explanations or instructions given to me by others.	I question accepted explanations and reasons and think of alternative ways to do things.	
	I consider the options before I decide on any action.	I act, speak or make decisions before I think through options.	
	I keep a tidy work area or room where I am working.	I spread out over a desk or room where I am working.	
	I prefer to do one task at a time and am stressed by having too many tasks at once.	I prefer to be involved in two, three or more tasks at a time.	
	Left Total	**Right Total**	

This can give you a very rough idea of whether you use both hemispheres equally, or if one is dominant over the other. In most people one hemisphere becomes dominant over the other and one side of the brain is used to process information more than another. (A similar example of hemisphere dominance is right or left handedness, though this does not correlate at all with hemisphere dominance in learning styles.)

This dominance means you will be better at some tasks than others. For instance,
- making and following a list of instructions is a left hemisphere task.
- thinking of new approaches to something is a right hemisphere task.

Ideally we should use our left side for left brain tasks and the right side for right brain tasks, but that is not the way it always works. When we have left school we tend towards activities that require the dominant side and away from activities that require the less dominant side. *Teaching and training would be much more effective if was offered to learners in both right and left sided ways of learning.* This is what we call *whole brain learning and teaching*.

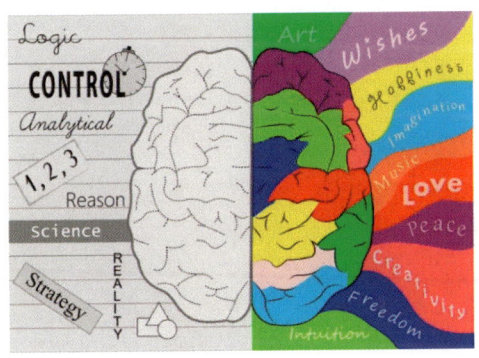

In Education

There is very strong evidence for the hemisphere differentiation, but there are many common misconceptions about right and left hemisphere functions as this image illustrates—for instance music, art, love and creativity on the right side! Lateralisation is usually in evidence by nine years of age. No-one grows up to be completely left or right dominant. Due to upbringing, education and work experiences an individual who is *naturally* right or left dominant can develop the abilities of the opposite hemisphere quite effectively. It is rare to find someone who is 50/50 in terms of left and right hemisphere features. It is also rare to find both partners in a marriage or a relationship who share the same dominance. In most relationships one partner is left dominant and the other right—with obvious applications in marriage guidance!

The education system in the UK *is strongly left hemisphere dominated* in the delivery of information and the assessment of learning. Information is delivered in a logical and sequential form in highly structured classroom contexts. Learning is expected to take place in a largely abstract environment where facts and information are delivered apart from a practical context or through appropriate experiences. It therefore favours left dominant learners and discriminates against young people who are right brain dominant. It is interesting to compare this with the outdated approach of forcing children to write with the right hand and not the left. Some of the methods used to coerce children to write with the right hand would now be considered as abusive. Yet the dominance of left brain approaches in teaching and learning as the *correct way* to teach and learn is just as problematic.

A practical application of this was researched in the EntreBRAINeur Study of 2010 (see www.stran.ac.uk/research) which demonstrated that a majority of entrepreneurs in the Study were *right dominant, non-conforming* learners. This means that in a left dominant education system they were discriminated against in the same way as left handed pupils used to be.

- Many young people who do not conform to the norms within a school setting are right dominant learners.
- Many adults who feel alienated from education are right dominant learners.

People with a dominance for one side can adjust to using the other side if they are motivated to do so. For instance,

i. to succeed at tasks they need to accomplish e.g. pass an examination.
ii. to engage in something they are very interested in.

Formal education involves a left-brain approach to learning. Years of constantly having to adapt can cause serious stress for a right dominant person as well as a sense of failure and of not 'fitting in'.

Some extremely right brain dominant young people can be misdiagnosed as having ADHD when, instead, they need to be taught in right brain ways i.e. *with the grain* of the brain. This subject is developed in *Right–brained Children in a Left-brained World* by Freed and Parsons (1997).

Lateralisation explains why
- some children regularly question explanations and instructions that others accept.
- some pupils always try to get people to conform to what they want to do rather than conform to what is expected of them.
- some pupils like to think through information before responding, while others respond on impulse.

Can you identify which hemisphere is being used in the following activities? Write R or L in the appropriate box. Then compare and discuss this with a friend.

	answering open ended questions (with no right/wrong answer)
	answering closed questions (with right/wrong answers)
	spontaneous discussion (without preparation)
	structured discussion (after individual preparation)
	in planning and devising a new project, activity etc.
	in following or implementing clear, systematic instructions for an activity
	re-presenting learned material in a test or examination
	maintaining a tidy working area
	understanding metaphors
	keeping more than one task going at a time
	giving a logical and systematic explanation or record
	using mindmaps
	making lists and systematic notes

Here is another practical exercise to try.

Which hemisphere preference is a pupil showing when he or she

	questions the purpose of an activity or what they are being taught?
	asks for more detail about how to do a task correctly?
	wants to be sure that they will be able to present their learning correctly?
	is motivated to work harder to get higher grades?
	challenges accepted ways of doing things and presents alternatives?
	pushes the boundaries of behaviour?
	reacts to other students who do not keep to rules and procedures?
	challenges standard procedures?
	needs time to reflect on answers before responding?
	day dreams?
	tries to get you or the other students to fit around them?

It can be very important to realise
- what your own hemisphere dominance is.
- what your partner's hemisphere dominance is.
- what dominance is favoured in your workplace.
- the hemisphere dominance of your boss or line-manager.
- what dominance you can identify in your children.

Here are three practical examples of how important this can be.

Example 1 In your work

Your hemisphere dominance may not match that of your boss or line manager, or may it may be similar to theirs. If you are right hemisphere dominant and your line manager is left dominant you may find that an emphasis on accountability, detailed reports and lack of opportunity to influence policy or processes is frustrating and de-motivating. If you are left dominant and have a right dominant boss, you may find be frustrated by the absence of detailed instructions, clear expectations and too much visionary thinking. Random unscheduled changes may leave you confused and de-motivated. However, if your manager or boss appreciates the value of your brain dominance, as something that complements his or her own dominance then there is potential for a very productive working relationship.

There is a similar potential for complementarity amongst work colleagues. If right dominant people are given tasks that utilise right hemisphere skills they will be happier and more productive. The opposite will be true if they are confined to left hemisphere tasks. The same will be true for left dominant employees. However, if each individual in the team is able to 'play to their strengths' and contribute their brain dominance to any project, there will be not only be more harmony but more productivity and creativity.

Example 2 For parents

Your children will probably display differences in right and left hemisphere dominance. A left dominant child will find the left dominant school system goes with the grain of his or her brain. They conform to the sequential methods of learning and accept explanations and procedures without question. They focus on doing their best within the parameters laid down for them. How do you think a parent-teacher interview about this child will go? Will it be pleasant and positive or negative and problematic?

A right dominant child will struggle with the left dominant approaches of school which go against the grain of the brain. He or she will think randomly and not sequentially and come up with answers without being able to explain how they arrived at them. They will question and challenge accepted explanations or procedures and want to know *why* certain things have to be done or studied. They challenge the parameters set for them to learn in. How do you think a parent-teacher interview about this child will go compared to the left dominant child?

Consider how the parents respond to the interview. It is possible that one child will be praised and commended while the other is corrected and told to conform more in the future. Then consider how the sibling that has been commended will be viewed by the one who is not.

Many right dominant children become alienated from formal education and school at an early age *because every day they are constantly being taught against the right hemisphere grain of the brain.* This is discouraging and de-motivating. It can lead to the child dis-engaging from education, experiencing conflict with parents and 'authority' figures, and to tension and resentment between siblings.

Example 3 For teachers
A left dominant teacher will 'teach by the book' and adhere to fixed and predictable routines, procedures and timetables. Pupils whose left hemisphere dominance responds well to these approaches will find themselves 'at home' with such a teacher. Right dominant pupils will struggle if their teachers do not recognise the difference between left and right dominance and how their personal teaching styles affects pupils who are right dominant, there will be conflict and tension with these pupils.

The same is true for right dominant teachers and left dominant pupils. However, since our education system is left dominant, right dominant students are arguably less likely to choose teaching as a career and more left dominant students will opt for teacher training. In most teacher training institutions they will then experience left brain dominant teacher training. Students who undertake a one year PGCE frequently do so after three years of a subject degree delivered in a left dominant approach.

During their training it is likely that they will not be taught about the implications of Lateralisation in the classroom. They will then graduate to teach in the left dominant education system, where they will be inspected and assessed on left brain criteria. The outcome of this is that right dominant pupils will rarely be taught by a right dominant teacher who will empathise with them and knows how to teach with the grain of their brains.

In my experience, many right dominant learners look back on their school experience and find that one or two teachers stood out as teaching with the grain of his or her brain. Unfortunately, these were the exception to the general rule.

Thus, it is imperative that teachers are trained to
- to recognise and identify their own hemisphere dominance.
- to realise how this influences the ways in which they teach.
- to recognise the features of left and right dominance in pupils.
- to identify which hemisphere they are seeking to engage when they ask pupils to perform specific skills and tasks.
- to adapt their teaching to left and right dominant learners.

On the following pages you will find a description of some characteristics of each hemisphere that parents and teachers may find helpful in identifying any dominance and catering for in teaching and learning.

If you are not a teacher you will be able to identify characteristics that will help you understand, and work harmoniously with, colleagues and friends.

Whether you are an employee, an employer, or a manager of people, you will find something in these descriptions that could be useful in working with people effectively and efficiently.

In *The Master and His Emissary (2009)*, Iain McGilchrist suggests helpful distinctions between the hemispheres. The *left hemisphere* is associated with narrow, focused attention and processes information that it can *re-present* as accurate and certain. This become a dominant 'reality' for the left hemisphere. The right hemisphere is associated with broad attention and processes information relative to what it perceives to be the *present* reality. It is less focused on factual accuracy and theory as much as on what actually works in practice.

Right Hemisphere Dominance

- Learn better when they *see a purpose* for learning something and are *reminded why* they are learning it.
- Enjoy being able to contribute their own ideas to a project and be involved in planning new ways of doing things.
- Need to be careful that they are not doing too many tasks that they cannot complete.
- Will not always accept the explanations or instructions they are given by others and need to be careful about how they challenge these.
- A teacher or parent who sticks to routines will frustrate them.
- Can have in instinct or 'gut feeling' about what to do—and often be right.
- May get the right answer without knowing how they got it.
- May need to learn to think more about what they say, or about decisions they make, before speaking or acting.
- May find it hard to be patient enough to receive complete instructions before getting on with work.

Left Hemisphere Dominance

- Learn better when they are given clear instructions and know exactly what is expected of them.
- Need to learn to ask for clear instructions when the instructions they have been given are too vague.
- A disorganised teacher, or one who changes plans without warning, will frustrate them.
- Prefer to do one task at a time. Too many tasks cause stress.
- Will hesitate to answer questions in class if not confident about having the correct answer. They should try to take more of a risk to speak before being sure they are correct or will not make a mistake.
- Need to learn to ask how they can find the information the teacher will be looking for *before* they have to take part in a group discussion.

Extreme Right Hemisphere Dominance

Some children have an extreme right dominance which means that they approach all tasks using right hemisphere abilities, even when they should use the left hemisphere. There is no clear dividing line between these children and children with ADD (Attention Deficit Disorder). Some children diagnosed as ADD are extreme right dominant learners, but most teachers are not taught to recognise these children, nor are they trained in how to teach them. If a child shows evidence of twelve or more of the following features, he or she is probably extremely right dominant.

1	Day dreams a lot.
2	Uses fingers to count.
3	Has difficulty following directions.
4	Is good at remembering places and events but not so good at names and numbers.
5	Often has a messy desk when working.
6	Works part-way out of a seat or standing up.
7	Has difficulty completing work on time.
8	Often gives the right answer to a question without being able to explain where it came from.
9	Tries to change the world around themselves.
10	Chews tongue or sticks it out of the mouth when working.
11	Draw pictures on the corners of worksheets.
12	Likes to learn in class by touching, handling and doing.
13	Likes to use imagination.
14	Not good at judging how long something will take to do.
15	Gives responses unrelated to what is being discussed.

This selection was taken from *Unicorns are Real* by Barbara Vitale, 1982. (Interestingly, children in the Autistic Spectrum often exhibit features of extreme left hemisphere dominance.)

Checklist

Here is the next Checklist. Once again, you might like to respond to these questions with a Y for yes and an N for no.

Are you left hemisphere dominant? Y or N
Are you right hemisphere dominant? Y or N
Are you neither, but use both hemispheres equally? Y or N
Do you recognise the impact of left or right hemisphere dominance in your workplace? Y or N
Can you see how it could impact your relationships with colleagues? Y or N
Could your brain dominance have an impact on your job satisfaction? Y or N
Do you recognise either left or right dominance in your children? Y or N
Do you see ways in which this influences how they learn or work? Y or N
Has this had an effect on their performance in school? Y or N

Top Tips!

Underline the tick if this statement is true for you already.
Circle the tick if you are intending to put this into practice.

- ✓ How did you score in the right and left hemisphere table? Would you try it out on someone else in your family?
- ✓ Complete the tables which describe right or left hemisphere activities. Compare it with someone else's answers.
- ✓ Use these descriptors to review your work contexts and colleagues? Take one or two people as examples.
- ✓ Use these descriptors to identify what kind of activities or tasks your own children or pupils struggle with. Can this be explained by a specific hemisphere dominance in them?
- ✓ Review the characteristics for left or right hemisphere dominance. Underline anything that might be helpful in helping your children or pupils learn with the grain of the brain.

CHAPTER 10

Cooperation or Conflict?

We have looked at the differences in the way people think and learn and we have seen that learning is not facilitated most effectively by a 'one size fits all' approach. Each of us needs to value the ways in which we learn as individuals rather than think there is one 'right way' to learn. We also learn better when our teachers understand this and know what to do about it.

We have looked at eight different *Smartnesses* and nine different *Sensory Preferences*. Many young adults who struggled with education tell me how much difference it would have made to their own school experience if they had been taught in the light of this. Would it have made a difference to you if this had been the approach in your school?

People not only *learn* in different ways, they also *prefer to work* in different ways. In this chapter we will look at four ways of working or *Working Styles*. These may help you see why you got on better with some teachers than others at school. They will also give you an insight into why you get on better with some people at work, or in friendships, than with others. People with the same Working Style as you will usually be easier to work with. You might find you clash with people who have other Working Styles. This can happen at work or with a partner or with your children when their Working Styles are different to yours. A number of similar approaches to this exist and in Fingerprint Learning we have drawn from various models, including the approach of Cynthia Tobias, who drew on the work of Anthony Gregorc's Mind Styles in adults. We have described the four different Working Styles in terms of *Boundaries* and these are summarized in the following boxes. Most people have features of each of these Working Styles, but are usually dominant in one or two. They reflect the different wiring of our brains or different 'grains of the brain'. If you are asked to work in a way that does not match your own Working Style, you may find you lose motivation and enthusiasm for the work. These boxes contain key phrases relating to each of the Working Styles.

Boundary Keeper
- ✓ Be clear about what you expect from me
- ✓ Don't be vague; give me a plan.
- ✓ Show me an example.
- ✓ Give me a reward for my work.

Boundary Pusher
- ✓ Give me enough time to finish.
- ✓ Appreciate the effort I have put in.
- ✓ Give me a greater challenge next.
- ✓ Where can I find out more?

Boundary Filler
- ✓ Who will I be working with?
- ✓ Will my friends be around?
- ✓ I try hard to please everybody.
- ✓ Is everyone getting along?

Boundary Breaker
- ✓ Is it necessary?
- ✓ Can it wait?
- ✓ I'm bored! Let's move on.
- ✓ What is the point of this?

Do you recognise yourself described in any of these boxes? Which of the boxes contain more descriptions of how you prefer to work?

Boundary Keepers

They like to know what the boundaries are in terms of what is expected of them. They do their best work when they
- have clear instructions..
- know what to expect.
- have routines to follow.
- are given clear rules.
- receive tangible rewards for their work—a prize, badge, wage.

What Boundary Keepers find difficult.

- Understanding what has not been clearly explained.
- Adjusting to unexpected change.
- Unfulfilled expectations.
- Interruptions to their work
- When others do not keep the rules.
- Not receiving a tangible or adequate reward for their work.

Boundary Pushers

They work to the edge of their boundaries, putting effort into what they enjoy doing. They do their best work when they
- have time to complete work to their own satisfaction.
- know the extra effort they put into work is appreciated.
- work on something they are personally interested in.
- they are rewarded by moving on to a harder challenge.

What Boundary Pushers find difficult.

- Pressure to complete work within a time limit.
- Others in a group not caring about a task as much as they do.
- Working on something they are not personally interested in.
- Repeating the same work with no progression.
- Being pushed to meet deadlines.

Boundary Fillers

They are motivated when the work context is filled with positive relationships and people are getting on together. They do their best work when they
- can work with others they get on with.
- have time for social interaction at work or school.
- are sure there is harmony in the work or family environment.
- feel they are getting along with a teacher or manager.

What Boundary Fillers find difficult.
- Working on their own without enough social interaction.
- Disharmony or tension in their group or family.
- When they are made to feel guilty about their work.
- When too many instructions or rules impede relationships.

Boundary Breakers

Motivated by moving on to something new and not being confined within boundaries. They do their best work when they
- are involved in planning new approaches to a task.
- have options about what work they do or how to do it.
- can question accepted ways and approaches.
- can keep moving on to something different or new.
- know *why* work is being done and why *now*.

What Boundary Breakers find difficult.
- Too much routine and lack of variety—repetition bores them.
- Going back over work they have missed or need to correct.
- Following rules—other's rules are 'guidelines' for them.
- Not being given options and choices.
- Working with a teacher, parent, manager or boss who sticks to strict routines and procedures.

(Their tendency to question accepted ways of doing things may misinterpreted as disrespectful, although it probably isn't.)

Can you recognise work colleagues, family members or pupils in these categories? Remember, although most people have characteristics of all four, they usually are dominant in one or two. Can you see how the different Working Styles can either cooperate or be in conflict with the others? For instance, here are some possible scenarios to consider.

1. *A parent who is a Boundary Keeper.*

Cooperation Scenario	Conflict Scenario
A child who is a *Boundary Keeper* will be happy to work with fixed routines and rules.	A *Boundary Breaker* child will challenge routines and question the reasons for doing work— and having to do it now!

2. *A teacher who is a Boundary Keeper.*

Cooperation Scenario	Conflict Scenario
A child who is a *Boundary Keeper* is secure because the teacher probably gives clear instructions/expectations for work.	The *Boundary Filler* child can feel that the teacher cares more about the work being done correctly than about him or her.

3. *A manager who is a Boundary Pusher.*

Cooperation Scenario	Conflict Scenario
Someone who is a *Boundary Pusher* will be motivated because the manager is not rushing him or her to complete work to a deadline.	A *Boundary Breaker* can feel the manager is interested only in completing the task but has not helped him or her to see a purpose for doing it.

Checklist

Here is a Checklist you might like to review by circling a Y for yes and an N for no.

Can you identify the four Working Styles in your family or friends? Y or N

Can you put the name of a person you know to each of these working styles? Y or N

If you are a teacher, can you put the name of a student to each of these? Y or N

Can you recall examples of where a clash between these styles caused conflict, not cooperation? Y or N

Top Tips for Working Styles

Underline the tick if this statement is true for you already.
Circle the tick if you are intending to put this into practice.

- ✓ Take some time to score yourself. Give yourself a 2, 1, or 0 for how strongly each category describes you.
  (2 = strong 1 = moderate 0 = weak).
- ✓ Try this out on colleagues or friends.
- ✓ Do the same exercise for your children.
- ✓ Go through the lists of what motivates them to do their best work and what they find difficult. Highlight the features that describe each individually.
- ✓ Work out how you can use this to produce greater co-operation and less conflict with individual pupils or children—or colleagues.

CHAPTER 11

Learning and Memory

Memory and memorising are fundamental to effective learning. If you cannot remember what has been taught, you cannot progress in learning. The connections we make between pieces of information must 'stick' if we are to add more connections to them and build networks. In terms of the brain, this means causing the neuronal connections to become permanent. This is what memory is about and it is something we all take for granted without thinking much about it.

Memory is vital to moving on to another Learning Cycle effectively because it embeds the progress made in the previous Learning Cycle and builds on it. In this chapter, I want to prompt you to think about memory and give some tips about how to use it more effectively in teaching and learning.

Most people are familiar with the three dimensions of memory and how they inter-relate. I liken these to the Children's Notepad, the Fridge and the Freezer, as the following paragraphs will explain.

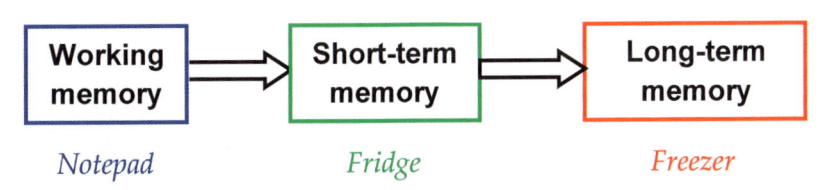

Working memory	→	Short-term memory	→	Long-term memory
Notepad		*Fridge*		*Freezer*

Working Memory is the memory we use to remember information for a very brief period of time. It is the memory you use when you remember the words being spoken in a sentence until the sentence has been completed and you have grasped what the speaker meant. You then clear the working memory to take in more information. If you didn't do this, your working memory would have too much information to process at once.

You may be aware of using your working memory when you keep repeating some information aloud, like a phone number, until you get the chance to write it down—and then you can safely forget it because it is recorded. I liken this to the 'magic' notepads used by children to write on with a plastic pencil and then remove what they wrote down by lifting the clear plastic sheet.

Short-term memory lasts longer. The initial goal of teaching is to transmit information in the *working memory* to the *short-term memory*. For instance, your short-term memory will recall some of the information you have been reading in this book while you read the chapter. After reading this particular chapter you may recall that there are three levels of memory—but you may not remember what they are. In other words, your working memory grasped what you have just read about the three levels and understood them, but only *the information that there are three levels* was transferred to your short-term memory—not what the three levels are. Transferring the information to your short-term memory takes some intentional effort or special interest. It also depends on what information was already in your *long term memory*. I liken the short-term memory to a fridge which preserves food from perishing for a limited period of time. However, if you want to preserve it for a long period you need to transfer it to the 'freezer' of long term memory.

Long-term memory is the memory where we store information for months and years. This is essential to learning because the ability to memorise new information depends on 'attaching' it to the information already stored in the long term memory. If information was not stored there already, then the working memory and short-term memory cannot not connect the new information with anything already embedded in the memory and learning will not take place.

When we are young, we are exercising our memories continually. When you watch a child playing you can observe how memory is being built as they repeat certain procedures or sounds. *Practice* and *repetition* is essential for embedding information in long-term memory and children do this automatically. However, for a right dominant person there must be variety in this process, whereas for a left dominant person the routine is helpful.

School involves an intensive use of our memories to retain information but when we leave school and begin to work this decreases significantly. We do not 'exercise' our memory as much as we had in the past and, since memory is like a muscle, the lack of practice weakens its resilience. We should be taking steps to keep it in peak condition, but most people take memory for granted rather than consciously exercising it. By the time we retire it has become lazy and, instead of exercising our memory to keep it fit, we live off what is already stored and embedded in long-term memory. Working memory and short-term memory are not being stimulated as much as they should be and so we are not adding to long-term memory, which becomes fixed. We find that our memory becomes inefficient and lets us down more frequently, but instead of doing something to counteract this we tend to accept this as an inevitable part of ageing—perhaps as 'senior moments'. It isn't!

Memory improves through exercise and use. 'Use it or lose it' is an appropriate phrase to employ in this context—for children as well as adults. There are some important facts about memory that can help you to improve your own memory, as well as the memory of your children or students. Among these facts is the existence of *five kinds of memory* involved in learning to which teaching can be directed. These five memories store information in complementary ways. Learning is most effective when it is targeted to *all five memories* and not just one or two. Some of these memories are stronger in some adults and children than in others. In teaching or *training it is important to know which memories you are targeting.* It also useful to identify which memories are weaker and which are stronger in an individual learner.

The following numbering for each memory will be used again at the end of this chapter.

1. Verbal-Phonological memory for *words, text, information.*

This is the memory that enables you to remember vocabulary, poetry, drama lines, and other information such as addresses and names. However, storing information in verbal memory does not mean the information is *understood*—only that is has been remembered. Putting information into rhyme or poetry is a very effective way of using verbal memory.

2. Visual-Spatial memory for *images, pictures and positioning.*

This memory enables you to remember pictures and images. It remembers information in a visual format, e.g. diagrams, flowcharts, and information that is highlighted in colour. It remembers faces and where something you have seen was positioned with reference to other things around it, e.g. in text, or images on a page. Some pupils with a poor verbal memory store information better in visual form. They should be encouraged to transfer verbal information to images or diagrams—or be given the information in that form in the first place.

3. Procedural *memory* for *procedures and sequences.*

This memory helps you remember sequences and procedures, such as in dance or drama or in working a gadget or machine. Poor procedural memory can be evident in forgetting to bring things to school or take them home. It can be helped by putting the sequential steps in any procedure into words or images so that other memories are employed to help the weaker one.

4. Semantic memory for *something you understand.*

This is the memory that remembers once it has understood what you are trying to remember. It is the key memory for learning. Someone to have a good semantic memory but a poor verbal memory. In other words, he or she can *understand* information but not *repeat it* in a specific form of words e.g. a poem.

5. Episodic memory for *recalling past events and incidents.*
This memory remembers events and incidents from the past and then recalls details about that event e.g. where you were when you heard about the Twin Towers. Information linked to events or incidents that are funny, ridiculous or sad is more easily remembered by children—and adults. Teachers can 'stage' memorable events that will create links to the information they are teaching.

If you are a teacher it is important to be aware of which of the five memories you are targeting in a particular lesson. You should try to reach all five memories in every subject you teach, even if you spread them over more than one lesson. An effective teacher will show their pupils how to create mnemonics and include creating these as homework or as a class project.

There are *two key principles* in helping all age groups use their memories to learn effectively. We continually use these principles without realizing that we do.

Association—This means linking pieces of information together. In the case of memory it means linking new information in your short-term memory to information *already in your long-term memory.* An example would be linking a new name to a person you already know, or connecting some new information to a tune you already know.

Imagination—This involves the use of images, which is a powerful method the brain employs for remembering information. The images are already in your long-term memory. When you attach the new information to these images they are easily recalled. The use of colour in text or diagrams is also a powerful way to embed information in the memory.

This brings us to the importance of **Mnemonics and Memory**. For centuries, before information was available in printed form, or when manuscript books were expensive and rare, learners became accustomed to the use of mnemonics for memorisation.

These were considered to be essential tools for effective learning and students were actually instructed in how to employ them. Today, mnemonics are an underestimated learning tool and, consequently, are very much neglected as effective ways of exercising memory for effective learning. The effectiveness of mnemonics lies in their use of *Association*. Visual mnemonics are particularly effective because they employ *Imagination* as well as Association. You could try out the following examples of mnemonics for yourself and then consider how they might be useful for your children or pupils.

Visual Mnemonics
These are useful for remembering lists, names and sequences.
- Linking a name to an object e.g. Harry—seeing the person in a hurry; Henry—surrounded by six wives!
- A memory 'theatre' e.g. choose eight objects in a room in your house in a sequential order. Associate information you want to remember with each object in order. Practice with three and build it up. Try it out for a shopping list.
- A mental 'movie' to link sequences e.g. linking visual images in a sequence. For instance, 'see' yourself or someone else doing the things you are trying to remember.

Verbal Mnemonics
These can take various forms, such a *rhyming* mnemonics and *acronyms*.

Rhyming Mnemonics
Here are two examples of rhyming mnemonics that many of us will be familiar with:

Thirty days hath September,
April, June, and November;
All the rest have thirty-one
Excepting February alone:
Which hath but twenty-eight days clear,
And twenty-nine in each leap year.

I before E, except after C is another rhyming mnemonic that most of us have used, although there are exceptions such as 'seize' and 'weir'!

You may have come across a variation of this as follows;:

I before E, except after C – and 'weird' is just weird.

Acronyms

This is a form of mnemonic we use frequently without realising it. In an acronym, information is abbreviated by using letters of other words and then pronouncing these as a word.

Here are examples of some spelling acronymns.

There's a **rat** in **separate**.

Because – **B**ig **E**lephants **C**an **A**lways **U**nderstand **S**mall **E**lephants.

Arithmetic – **A** **R**at **I**n **T**he **H**ouse **M**ay **E**at **T**he **I**ce **C**ream.

Rhythm – **R**hythm **H**elps **Y**our **T**wo **H**ips **M**ove.

You may have come across something similar in recalling musical notation by Every Good Boy Deserves Fun for **EGBDF**.

In the UK, many of us remember the colours of the rainbow by using the following mnemonic:

Richard Of York Gave Battle In Vain
for
Red, Orange, Yellow, Green, Indigo, Violet.

These are simple to make up and can be great fun for children and young people. Of course, when you make up a mnemonic of your own you will remember it better.

Musical Mnemonics

This is also useful for lists. Put the information you want to remember to a tune you already know. The tune is already in your long term memory and the new information 'attaches' to it. Children often use musical mnemonics to learn the alphabet, i.e. abcdefg. I learnt the bells of London in the song 'Oranges and Lemons' — and cannot forget it, even though I have no use for it!

Kinaesthetic Mnemonics

Move your body to remember sequences. For instance, move a different part of your body to recall a different piece of information. Practice a procedure you need to remember repeatedly until it lodges in your memory e.g. turning off electric switches at night.

Do you think you could learn to count from one to five in Japanese in 5 minutes? You can, with the following mnemonic that combines visual, verbal and kinaesthetic features. I cannot recall where I was introduced to this but it stuck in my memory!
The first five numbers in Japanese are
1 - ichi 2 - ni 3 - san 4 - shi 5 - go.

For a *verbal mnemonic* translate these as
ichi = itchy
ni = knee
san = sun (North American pronunciation!)
shi = she
go = go

Next, turn this into a *kinaesthetic mnemonic.*
Ichi ni = itchy knee = scratch your knee as you say it.
San = sun = point to the sky.
Shi = she = stroke your hair as if it was long like a girl's.
Go = walk = walk on the spot.
This becomes a *visual mnemonic* when you *imagine yourself* doing the action instead of actually moving. You can make this a *musical mnemonic* by putting the five words to a tune e.g. Itchy knee, Itchy knee, sun she go; sun she go, to the first line of *Frere Jacques*.

There are so many ways to be creative in making up mnemonics for your children. They can be fun to do and the process of inventing them embeds them in their memories. Google **Mnemonics** to find information and resources for more ideas on mnemonics for your children—or yourself.

Checklist for Memory
Here are some questions for the Checklist on Memory.
Do you think you use your memory as much as you did when you were younger? Y or N
Do you see the difference between working, short-term and long-term memory? Y or N
Circle which of the five memories are your strongest.
                    1 2 3 4 5
Circle which of the five memories are your weakest.
                    1 2 3 4 5
Which of the five memories do you use most in your work?
                    1 2 3 4 5
Can you recognize how your children use each of the five memories to learn? Y or N
Can you recall any mnemonics you learnt in school to remember information? Y or N
Do your children use mnemonics for learning? Y or N.
Have you tried teaching them to create mnemonics for themselves? Y or N

Top Tips for Memory.
Underline the tick if this statement is true for you already.
Circle the tick if you are intending to put this into practice.
- ✓ I use mnemonics to remember information myself.
- ✓ As a teacher I use mnemonics to help my pupils remember information.
- ✓ As a teacher I know which of the five memories I am targeting in my lessons.
- ✓ As a parent I show my children how to create mnemonics to remember information.
- ✓ I look out for new ideas for creating mnemonics to keep my memory fit.

CHAPTER 12

Let's *Do* Something *Now!*

"Teaching without doing is like making love without touching."
Barbara Prashnig, The Power of Diversity, 2008.

I hope you have enjoyed this introduction to whole brain learning and have learnt more about your own *learning fingerprint*. Our brains are truly amazing and the individuality of how your brain is wired for learning is part of your uniqueness. I believe strongly that the role of teaching in any context—work, home or school—should include helping each learner realise this uniqueness and value it. My journey of discovery about how individual brains are wired for learning has transformed my own life as well as my approach to teaching. It has been my privilege to share some of this through this manual.

If you are a *learner* I hope you have discovered how to learn more effectively in the future—and why you might have struggled, or failed, in the past. Knowing how to employ the grain of your brain for your advantage could make all the difference to your professional development in work, college or university.

If you are a *teacher or parent* I hope you have discovered ideas to put into practice as you teach your pupils or children with the grain of their brains.

Most of what you have read in this book is not yet considered to be a fundamental part of teacher training or daily teaching practice. This is not the fault of teachers. Indeed I have found teachers are eager to understand and apply what I been presenting as 21st century whole brain teaching. The problem appears to lie with our Education System that is still in 20th century 'suitcase carrying' mode as regards the delivery of teaching and the assessment of learning.

Top-down or bottom-up?
This means that a top-down revolution in teaching and learning is unlikely. But does this mean that the learning revolution is destined to pass us—and our children—by? I don't believe this is so if enough of us are convinced that we can do something to promote the revolution where we are now. Until there is a change in education policy schools, teachers and parents can still engage in promoting a learning revolution through whole brain approaches to teaching and learning.

Parents
can begin in the family with their children and they can encourage schools to get involved in whole brain teaching.

Youth Workers and *Training Organisations*
can use the insights of whole brain learning to show young people, who think they have failed in education, that *education may have failed them* by insisting that they learn against the grain of the brain and assessing them in ways that do not take account of their differences.

Teachers
can experiment with how to apply whole brain learning in their day to day teaching while still fulfilling the official assessment criteria, which do not yet reward them for innovative approaches to teaching with the grain of the brain.

School and College Principals and Management
can inspire and train their teaching staff for whole brain learning and develop them as *practitioners of learning* as well as of teaching.

Lifelong Learning Hubs

The rich resource of learning practitioners in the teaching profession could lead to schools and colleges becoming 'hubs' for learning in their communities. Parents, community workers, senior citizens and others could be introduced to lifelong, whole brain learning through such hubs. Whole communities could be transformed as people discover how to learn in ways that match the grain of their brains and that learning is for living and for life.

Schools and Colleges are more than 'qualification factories'. Just as *Health Centres* do not only deal with sickness but promote health within the whole community, Schools and Colleges could be *Learning Centres* that promote lifelong learning throughout the community. Understanding the brain and its amazing capacity to learn would have to be central to this project because it is central to learning. It can transform how people think about themselves as learners. I have seen this happen so many times. In Fingerprint Learning workshops we have discovered that people from the ages of ten to ninety do not find what you have read in this manual beyond their grasp, but are really interested to learn more. But where can they go to do so? Why not to Learning Centres with Learning Practitioners i.e. Schools and Colleges? This would indeed be a learning *revolution* on a community-wide scale.

The impact of lifelong learning on reducing the incidence of dementia, depression and social isolation (with its attendant health problems) would be incalculable if the older generation *was accustomed to cognitive stimulation* through 'learning hubs' that attracted them into lifelong learning on site or even by learning coming to them. For instance, a community learning hub could train people how to maintain a health memory through regular Memory Clubs or classes. Since memory lapses are a major cause for anxiety in older people and those who are close to them, why not engage learning practitioners to address this by training them how to *use their memory* instead of *losing it*?

Stranmillis University College have been offering a popular Lifelong Learning Programme in recent years and has clearly demonstrated that there is demand for this, so why should access to lifelong learning not be available *in every community where there are schools and colleges*? How many more people could be engaged in learning for life. If such programmes included the information on *whole brain learning* and *how to learn* presented in this manual it could be transformative as well as revolutionary.

Dream on!
Some people might consider me to be a dreamer for having a vision for Learning Centres on this scale and that it is completely impossible. I wonder if the concept of a local Health Centre would have seemed like an impossible dream a few generations ago when there was no National Health Service? Sceptics may well be right and this dream may be completely unreachable due to various obstacles. However, this does not mean there cannot be a learning revolution in your work or family, school or college class, youth group or residential home. *It can take place whenever someone is prepared to do something where they are now about what they have read in this manual—and share it with others.*

So, whether you are an individual learner, a teacher or a parent I hope you will now be equipped to understand, embrace and apply your personal learning preferences. I also hope you will be able recognize the learning preferences of those you nurture, teach, train or work alongside. It can make all the difference when you, and they, learn and work with the grain of the brain. Happier relationships develop in work, school or home when you work or teach with the grain of others' brains. If you put what you have learnt about whole brain learning into practice, you will be challenging the status quo where you are—and helping to advance the *Learning and Teaching Revolution*. I hope, as you finish this book, you feel inspired to do so—and that you will continue to use it as a practical manual in your day to day experience.

Thank you for reading it!

Further Reading

Baddeley,A., Your Memory, A User's Guide, Prion Books, London, 2002.
Buzan, T,. Mindmaps for Kids, Thorsons, 2003.
Campbell, L., Campbell, B., Dickinson, D., Teaching and Learning through Multiple Intelligences, Allyn& Bacon, Boston, 1996.
Dryden, G, and Vos, J. The New Learning Revolution, Continuum Books, London , 2005.
Dunn, Rita and Ken, Teaching Students through their Individual Learning Styles; A Practical Approach, Reston Publishing Co.1978.
Dunn, Rita, and Griggs, Shirley, A., Learning Styles: A Quiet Revolution in American Schools, Reston, VA: National Association of Secondary School Principals, 1998.
Fleetham, M., Multiple Intelligences in Practice, Network Continuum Education, Stafford, 2006
Freed, J. and Parsons, L., Right-brained Children in a Left-brained World, Simon and Schuster, New York, 1997.
Gardner, H., Frames of Mind: The Theory of Multiple Intelligences, Basic Books, New York, 2011.
MacGilchrist, I., The Master and His Emissary, Yale University Press, 2009.
Norden,J., Understanding the Brain, Virginia, The Teaching Company, 2007.
Prashnig, B., The Power of Diversity, Network Educational Press, Stafford, 2008.
Restak,R., Optimizing Brain Fitness, Virginia, The Teaching Company, 2007.
Cummins B. and Kelly J., The EntreBRAINeur Study, 2010, www.stran.ac.uk
Tobias, C.U., The Way They Learn, Wheaton, Illinois, Tyndale House, 1994.
Tobis, C.U., Every Child Can Succeed, Colorado, Focus on the Family, 1996.
Vitale, B. M., Unicorns are Real, Torrance, CA, Jalmar Press, 1982.

The Fingerprint *Learning for Life* Programme

These Workshops explain differences in the ways people learn, how to overcome barriers due to past educational experiences and how to teach and learn with the grain of the brain. Participants discover their individual 'grain of the brain' and practical steps they can take for successful learning and teaching in the future.

Workshop 1 How are you Smart?
- Smartnesses, employability and career selection.
- Eight ways of being smart.
- Find out in how many ways you are smart.
- How your smartnesses can help you find a job and choose a career.

Workshop 2 How the Brain Learns.
- How your brain learns.
- What stops your brain learning?
- Discover the 'grain of your brain'.
- How fears and threats prevent learning.
- The teenage brain.
- How to complete a 'Learning Cycle' for success in life.

Workshop 3 Sensory Preferences in Learning.
- How does the brain receive information? .
- Visual, Auditory, Tactile and Kinaesthetic sensory preferences.
- What are your own sensory learning preferences?
- How to use your sensory preferences to learn successfully.

Workshop 4 Working Styles and Right/Left Brain Learning
- Are you a Boundary Keeper, Pusher, Filler or Breaker?
- Right and Left Brain — which side of your brain is stronger?

Workshop 5 Individual Learning Profile and Tools for Learning
- Presenting Individual Learning Profiles for each participant.
- How to apply this to the Learning Cycle
- Building your own Learning Toolkit.

A Progressive Primary School Learning Plan

A progressive approach to Learning Styles in Primary School building up an Individual Learning Profile to be transferred to Post-Primary school with each pupil. (GB classes in brackets)

3rd year Primary (GB Y2)
How am I Smart? (not How Smart am I?)
- Profiling individual pupils for the eight smartnesses.
- Application to pupils' learning by the teachers.
- Developing all eight smartnesses in each child,
- Introducing parents to 'How is your child smart?' instead of 'How smart is your child?'

4th and 5th year Primary (GB Y3&4))
How do I take Information in? (Sensory Learning Preferences)
- Nine sensory preferences (VATK).
- Profiling individual pupil's sensory learning preferences.
- Application to pupils' learning by the teachers.
- Introducing sensory preferences to parents to help them work with their children.

6th year Primary (GB Y5)
Right and Left Hemisphere Dominance
- Identify right and left hemisphere characteristics.
- Profiling pupils for right left hemisphere dominance.
- Application to pupil learning by teachers.
- Introducing parents to right and left dominance.

Primary 7 (GB Y6)
Review Smartness and Career Selections and Working Styles
- Re-assess Smartnesses and linking to career selections..
- Profiling pupils for their working styles.
- Application to pupils' learning by teachers.
- Introducing parents to these working styles to equip them to engage with their children's education.

A Progressive Post-primary School Learning Plan

A progressive approach to Learning Styles in Post-primary School building up an Individual Learning Profile in preparation for GCSE studies. (GB classes in brackets)

Year 8 (GB Y7)
How am I Smart?
- Workshop for students on the eight smartness to identify 'How am I smart?' instead of 'How smart am I?'.
- Profiling individual students for their smartnesses.
- Application to pupil learning by the teachers.
- Linking these to career aspiration and school subjects.
- Introducing parents to 'How is your child smart?' instead of 'How smart is your child?'

Year 9 (GB Y8)
How do I take Information in? (Sensory Learning Preferences)
- Workshops for students on sensory learning preferences.
- Profiling individual students for their learning preferences.
- Application to learning and study/revision by the teachers.
- Workshop for parents on learning preferences to help them engage with children's learning.

Year 10 (GB Y9)
Right and Left Hemisphere Dominance and Working styles
- Workshops for students on right and left hemisphere dominance and working styles.
- Profiling students for right and left hemisphere dominance.
- Profiling individual working styles.
- Learning and study/revision applications by teachers.
- Workshops for parents.

In Year 10 (GB Y9) the completed learning profile can be used in the selection of GCSE subjects and potential career options.

Year 11, 12 (GB Y10,11) repeat smartnesses and careers profiles for A level selection.

NOTES

NOTES

NOTES

ABOUT THE AUTHOR

Dr. John Kelly graduated in Medicine from Queen's University Belfast in 1974. He is the Founder and Director of Fingerprint Learning Limited, an Education and Learning Consultancy, which is engaged in researching and developing applications of whole brain learning for all age groups in the spheres of Education, Business and Health.

The Fingerprint *Learning for Life Programmes* train individuals, parents, teachers and trainers in whole brain learning and Fingerprint Learning also profiles individuals for their personal learning styles. Fingerprint Learning provides assistance in developing progressive school programmes for whole brain learning and teaching.

John, with Dr. Brian Cummins of Stranmillis University College, Belfast, co-authored The EntreBRAINeur Study (Phase 1) into the Learning Preferences of Entrepreneurs in Northern Ireland (2010) and the Phase 2 Study (2014) into Entrepreneurial Education in Further Education Colleges. (See www.stran.ac.uk). Based on this research, he has developed the *Entrepreneurial Learning Inventory* which identifies entrepreneurial potential in individuals for successful commercial or social enterprise.

He has also developed the *BrainFit Programme* and *BrainFit Plan* for the prevention and delay of dementia, as well as *BrainFit Connect* for dementia therapy.

John and his wife Jenny live in Bangor, Northern Ireland, where Jenny practises as a Personal Image Consultant. They have four children and, at present, four grandchildren.

For further information on Fingerprint Learning resources and programmes see www.fingerprintlearning.com
or contact info@fingerprintlearning.com

Made in the USA
Charleston, SC
09 May 2016